Suzy's

A coffee house history

Susette Goldsmith

Quill

Published by Quill
www.quill.gen.nz

ISBN 978-0-473-17318-0
First published 2010

Every effort has been undertaken to source permission from the copyright holders to photographs and quotations included in this book.

Edited by Jeanette Cook, Nelson
Translations by Hans Hofkens, Paraparaumu
Designed by Jennie Aitken-Hall, Hall of Design, Oakura
Printed by Graphic Press & Packaging Ltd., Levin
Distributed by Greene Phoenix Marketing

Cover: Rita Angus, *At Suzy's Coffee Lounge* (1967), oil on hardboard; 500mm x 890mm, private collection, courtesy of the Estate of Rita Angus, image courtesy of Museum of New Zealand Te Papa Tongarewa.
Author photograph: Jane Dove Juneau ©

The history of coffee houses ...

was that of the manners,

the morals and the politics

of a people.

Curiosities of Literature, Isaac D'Israeli (1798)

Contents

Acknowledgements

First I must thank Suzy van der Kwast who trusted me enough to tell me her story and was sufficiently brave to remember the hard parts. I thank Tom too who encouraged us both to begin and later complete the project, and added his own thoughtful and good-humoured perspective.

Many people have assisted with this book in different ways and in particular I thank: Fritz Eisenhofer; Helen Eisenhofer; Katja Hilberink; Muriel Hoedermaekers; Rosalyn Hoedermaekers; Jo Link; William McAloon; Jan McGuinness; Stan Noble; Alan Perry and Luba Perry.

Staff members of Te Papa, the National Library and Wellington City Archives have been efficient and helpful in tracing image sources. Any mistakes or omissions are my own.

For permission to reproduce art work I am very grateful to Chris Mace and Dayle Mace, Bill Angus and the Estate of Rita Angus.

Jennie Aitken-Hall has generously provided services well beyond those of book designer and has been constant in her enthusiasm for the project. Paul Greenberg and Anna Hunt have willingly taught me much about the book trade.

For their very practical help and amused interest I thank Celia Goldsmith, Rupert Goldsmith and Katie Blackstock. To Paul, as always, thank you.

Next page: Joan Gillies created this energetic cover of the 5 December 1951 farewell dinner menu at The French Maid Coffee House. (Eph-b-dining-1951-01-front, Alexander Turnbull Library, Wellington.)

for
'double-quick'
service ..
EXHIBITIONS.
J.G.
The French Maid Coffee House....

Introduction

The day Suzy's Coffee Lounge opened Wellington took something of a jolt. Not of the seismic variety — which, in a city prone to earthly vibrations might have excited only resignation among its citizens — but a jolt of the caffeine type, an impulse that might raise one's blood pressure, quicken one's heart and kick-start one's brain.

There was no mention of the event in the *Evening Post,* or its morning equivalent *The Dominion,* and the city authorities, more concerned with matters of hygiene, health and safety than social change, neglected to celebrate their newest 'eating house'.

But the people in Wellington's streets knew. Urban osmosis — that intangible and powerful process that bubbles through office corridors and staff-rooms, percolates through shops and sports-grounds and stirs the air of book-clubs and living-rooms — had spread the word. And from the moment the Willis Street doors opened until the day they finally closed 23 years later, Suzy's was the place to be.

It was the 1960s, a time when for many New Zealanders coffee was routinely 'instant' or a dark brew of coffee essence — liquid coffee and chicory — suspended in hot milk, and a meal out was a rare treat and confined to tearooms (predominantly frequented by females), pubs (predominantly by males) or restaurants that offered few choices, no alcohol and an early night. Good service of the time simply meant plenty of food on the plate, clean fingernails on the waitress and the correct change.

The city was not completely devoid of sophistication, however, and Suzy's wasn't the first coffee bar in Wellington.

The French Maid was one of the earliest, opening on Lambton Quay in the 1940s. The Espresso Coffee Bar had opened on the Stewart Dawson corner in 1956 with a gleaming silver espresso machine from the Milan Trade Fair. Also on Lambton Quay, above Roy Parson's bookshop, a sophisticated European-style coffee bar had opened in 1957 and was run by Harry Seresin, a German-born son of Russian Jewish parents.

These pioneering coffee bars had grown out of other popular culinary institutions — the long, narrow and dazzlingly shiny milk bars of the 1930s that had emigrated from the United States and flourished with the stationing of American troops in Wellington during World War II. Greek immigrant D. Pagonis opened the Black and White in 1936 at 64 Willis Street and the Milky Way, at 4 Manners Street, was set up shortly after; they were followed by the Popular Milk Bar at 13 Courtenay Place, the Golden Gate at 78 Courtenay Place and the Rose at 222 Lambton Quay. One small milk bar attached to the Opera House continued trading until late 1999; and at least four of the earliest milk bars in the central city were owned and operated by the Tip Top dairy company, which introduced hokey-pokey to the sundae flavours choice. They were exciting meeting places that throbbed to the beat of garish, revving juke boxes.

There had been tearooms too, inherited from Britain and liberating women from compulsory male chaperoning. The new, noisy milk bars that had succeeded them became the modern stamping ground of young, clinging couples and, after school, teenagers testing parental boundaries.

It was the coffee bars, however, with their rich aromas of real coffee, thick palls of cigarette smoke, venerable coffee-house history and often fascinating accents that provided the grown-up havens which transformed hitherto grey and drab Wellington into a bright city with a vibrant café culture.

By whatever name it goes — coffee bar, coffee lounge, coffee shop, coffee house or café — each purveyor devoted to satisfying the needs of coffee drinkers is part of a noble trade with a long and intriguing history.

Coffee as a drink was first used as a medicine in the 15th century Arab world and later as a means to remain mentally alert during night-long religious sessions. It was drunk regularly in the Sufi monasteries in special ceremonies preceding the *dhkir* or ritual remembrance of the glory of God. The members of the Sufi orders passed the communal, red clay bowl of coffee to the right as they chanted their prayers. After its contents had been shared by the devotees, the bowl was passed to the lay members of the congregation.

Naturally enough, the many laymen at these sessions, while first linking the drink inextricably to the rites of religion, increasingly enjoyed what they drank. Turning its back on its purely religious associations, therefore, coffee leaked out of the monasteries of the Yemen into secular use in Islamic homes and then, most significantly, spilled into the *kahwe khaneh* — the first coffee houses.

And it's here that this story really begins.

Like the patrons of the Arabian coffee houses, Wellingtonians were quick to adapt to this new attraction. By day, the coffee bars' eager customers were office workers and professionals, city shoppers and university students. At night the intimate spaces offered a place to go after the movies, an excuse to dawdle, read the newspaper and smoke a cigarette, or an opportunity to argue a point, further a romance or avoid going home.

For the many new citizens who had fled Europe in search of a new and safe life they represented homes-away-from-home with their echoes of culture and sophistication. There was a 'European-ness' about Wellington's coffee bars with their brightly painted walls. Some sported posters of Spanish bull-fighting, others favoured prints of European scenes; many were draped with fishing nets and hung with floats and driftwood. Lighting was characteristically dim and provided by ubiquitous wine bottles stuffed with flickering candles that dripped on the small, often Formica, tables, threatening the hessian-covered walls and causing the city authorities much alarm. All the coffee bars were crowded, busy, noisy and popular.

Only one coffee bar, however, boasted young, Dutch émigré Suzy.

Starting Out

In all the great men's houses, there are servants whose business it is only to take care of the coffee; and the head officer among them, or he who has the inspection over all the rest, has an apartment allowed him near the hall which is destined for the reception of visitors. The Turks call this officer Kavveghi, that is, Overseer or Steward of the Coffee. In the harem or ladies' apartment in the seraglio, there are a great many such officers, each having forty or fifty Baltagis under them, who, after they have served a certain time in these coffee-houses, are sure to be well provided for, either by an advantageous post, or a sufficient quantity of land. In the houses of persons of quality likewise, there are pages, called Itchoglans, who receive the coffee from the stewards, and present it to the company with surprising dexterity and address, as soon as the master of the family makes a sign for that purpose, which is all the language they ever speak to them.

Arabic manuscript, Bichivili (16th century)

Probably, the New Zealand immigration official at The Hague had never heard of the *Kavveghi* or the luxurious coffee houses of Constantinople.

Possibly, like most New Zealanders in the 1960s, he rarely went out for dinner and, rather than coffee, regularly drank tea.

Certainly, he was surprised at the confident reply given by the young Dutch applicant to his standard question, ‘What do you want to do when you get to New Zealand?’

‘I want to be a waitress,’ Suzy said.

‘Oh yes. Why?’ the official asked.

‘I like serving people.’

The official seemed amused.

Well, you’ll have no problem finding work in New Zealand then. Kiwis aren’t too keen on serving other people. So, that’s up to you.’

She was accepted straight away.

Susanna Bekhuis was 21 when she left the Netherlands for New Zealand. It was a pleasant train-journey from her hometown, Almelo, to the port at Amsterdam, and her older brother Gerard came along for the ride. Her father Hendrikus found time on the journey for last minute advice: ‘Don’t spend all your money in the first week; don’t forget to take out health insurance as soon as you get there.’

Immigrating as well, and part of the Bekhuis family travelling party, was Suzy’s boyfriend Joop who had informed the officials in The Hague that he intended to open a restaurant in New Zealand.

Hendrikus had been taken aback by his daughter's announcement that she planned to emigrate to Australia. He already had two sons in New Zealand — Willy and Jan — and he was very reluctant to have Suzy disappear to the other side of the world too. Suzy had made up her mind, however, and she was going whether he liked it or not.

'But not until you're 21,' Hendrikus decreed.

'Why Australia?' Willy and Jan had wanted to know.

Because there are more people there so there must be better opportunities,' Suzy reasoned from Almelo.

'Don't go there, Suze,' came the reply from Invercargill. 'They're all criminals. New Zealand has a far better class of people. They're from Scotland.'

So she had modified her destination. She would be a waitress in New Zealand.

The familiar Dutch landscape raced by as the train slid towards Amsterdam. Village, fields, trees, village, fields, town, trees, village, fields, town ... Inside the carriage, Suzy sat up straight, alert, willing the train to hurry, wanting to begin the adventure. The train began to lose speed, running out of countryside and dawdling beside houses and gardens and shops and warehouses.

Amsterdam.

Moored in the port, the *Johan van Oldenbarnevelt* was simmering like an Arabian coffee pot. Excited young Dutch immigrants were aboard and heading to the other side of the world. Their parents huddled protectively around them. Introductions were made. Instructions were given. More instructions were given. Second thoughts hovered briefly in the air and were briskly brushed away by anticipation of the enormous adventure to come.

Some of the families elected to sail with their children as far as the final lock, the last point of home soil before the ship entered the North Sea. Hendrikus and Gerard were among them, and they sat with Suzy and Joop in the lounge, postponing the moment of separation. They drank coffee together and watched the parade of people jostling back and forth, organising luggage, exchanging addresses and locating cabins as the big ship gathered herself together for the voyage. They smoked cigarettes.

They made polite, nervous conversation. 'If you want to come back to Holland,' Hendrikus told his daughter, 'I expect you to fly your own plane.'

The ship forged on through the harbour; and then, as the last sea lock was reached and there was no more time, and final farewells began, something in Hendrikus snapped. It was all too much. He clutched his young daughter, crying bitterly and unable to let her go. He might never see her again. He wept. Suzy tried to to placate him. 'You've got all the other children ...' But he was inconsolable.

'You are my little princess,' he sobbed.

People stared and shifted uncomfortably as Hendrikus, now clearly out of control and growing more desperate, clung determinedly on to her.

It took the efforts of several men and a sincere promise from the ship's captain to take special care of this precious daughter to bustle Hendrikus off the ship. With all visitors now ashore, the *Johan van Oldenbarnevelt* headed steadily out to sea and towards Southampton, and her father's little princess, with £10 in her purse, frightened and severely shaken had gone.

Suzy sailed to New Zealand on the Johan van Oldenbarnevelt *on 11 April 1960. She is pictured (above) near the ship in Amsterdam on her last day in the Netherlands and (below) en route to the first stop at Southampton.*

Perhaps his young, strong-willed daughter was his favourite. Maybe he saw in her something of himself. Whatever the situation, the bond between Hendrikus and Suzy was a strong one.

Hendrikus Bekhuis was the youngest of four children. Family records name his grandfather as Jan Bekhuis from Tubbergen in the Dutch province of Overijssel, who was born in 1811 and married Johanna Dykhuis. They had three children, the oldest of whom, born in 1854, was the younger Hendrikus Bekhuis's father and bore the same name. His sister and brother were named Aleida and Johannes.

Hendrikus senior was a farmer in Tubbergen. His wife, Johanna Reinerink, was married twice, so young Hendrikus (born on 30 September 1896), Hendrika, Johannes and Gerhardus had four stepsisters.

A family story tells how Suzy's father met her mother, Catharina, when he was delivering two sacks of mail to the chief post office in Almelo. He worked as a postman, carrying the mail on the carrier at the front of his bicycle. He also owned a small farm nearby at Albergen. Catharina Bruinsma at the time worked in a drapery store in Almelo.

Both families were Roman Catholic. Catharina Bruinsma's great, great grandfather Willem Meijer (1816–1906) had escaped to Holland from Germany, where he had been held prisoner as a Catholic among Protestants. With his wife Zwaantje Huitema he had a son Huite Williems

Meijer who married Jantje Barkes De Vries and lived in Friesland. Their son Bouke Meijerwas born in Enzen Germany and married Hermina Bouwhuis. Their daughter — Suzy's grandmother — Catharina Meijer married a farmer, Wopke Bruinsma, who farmed first at the Pook in Twente and later at Schinnen in Limberg. Their daughter Catharina had two sisters (Johanna and Susanna) and five brothers (Sake Zacharis, Heronymus Antonius, Willem, Bouke and Jan), and was born on 15 July 1900, also in Enzen. She married Hendrikus Bekhuis on 11 August 1925 at St Mary's Church, Hoensbroek in Limberg.

Hendrikus was a tall, handsome man with large hands who reputedly could kill a rabbit for dinner with a single two-fingered blow. Catharina was a serene beauty with waist-length hair. This attractive young couple set up house together on the Albergen farm and immediately began their family. Twins arrived in April the next year, but only Hendrikus (Henny) Wilhelmus survived. His sister Catharina Anna died of pneumonia in 1927 at almost 10 months old. Two months after his sister's death Wilhelmus (Willy) Johannes was born.

Gerardus (Gerard) Antonius was born in 1928, Anna (Annie) Maria in 1930, Catharina (Toos) Suzanna in 1932 and Maria (Marietje) Wilhelmina in 1933. The next year, unnamed twins were stillborn. Hesina (Sieny) Johanna arrived in 1935 and twins Elizabeth (Betsy) Theresia and Johannes (Jan) Aloysius were born in 1936.

In that same year, and prophetically on Ash Wednesday, the young family's home burnt down. The fire began in the chimney early in the morning while Hendrikus and Catharina were at church in Albergen. Henny, Willy, Gerard, Annie, Toos, Marietje and Sieny were all at home. Their neighbours saw the fire, raised the alarm, took the children out of the house and released the horses. The frightened parents raced home on their bicycles to comfort their children and salvage what they could.

They started again, building a new and comfortable house that was spacious enough for a large family. Downstairs were the lounge, with steps up to an *opkammer* — a space for peace and quiet — and a huge kitchen with two dining tables, a stove and a hob. Below the *opkammer* was a cellar for storing fruit and vegetables over winter.

A door led on to an adjoining stable called the *deel,* with its water pump, large tub and washing machine and hayrick above, and the bathroom was nearby.

Upstairs were double bedrooms. Hendrikus who in his 40s had been diagnosed with a heart condition, later ritually climbed these stairs 10 times each morning and each evening on his doctor's orders.

Beyond the *deel* were the sheds for the pigs and the chickens and for packing the vegetables and fruit. Tall walnut trees grew in front of the house, and ivy soon began to climb up its walls.

Suzy was born, after the new house was built, on 2 September 1938. Her mother named her Susanna Maria after her own sister, and her family called her Suze. She was the 13th child born in the family; Catharina was 38 years old and had been married for just 13 years. Large numbers of children were not unusual for the times or for the Bekhuis family — Hendrikus's brothers Johannes and Gerhardus had both had 12 children — and Catharina was a good Catholic wife.

Next page: The Bekhuis family in 1947 outside their Albergen home are (from left back) Gerard, Betsy, Toos, Marietje, Willy, Sieny, Jan (from left front) Annie, Tony, Hendrikus, Herman, Trees, Catharina, Suzy and Henny.

In the beginning

With every cup of coffee you drink, you partake of one of the great mysteries of cultural history. Despite the fact that the coffee bush grows wild in highlands throughout Africa, from Madagascar to Sierra Leone, from the Congo to the mountains of Ethiopia, and may also be indigenous to Arabia, there is no credible evidence coffee was known or used by anyone in the ancient Greek, Roman, Middle Eastern, or African worlds. Although European and Arab historians repeat legendary African accounts or cite lost written references from as early as the sixth century, surviving documents can incontrovertibly establish coffee drinking or knowledge of the coffee tree no earlier than the middle of the fifteenth century in the Sufi monasteries of the Yemen in southern Arabia.

The World of Caffeine: the science and culture of the world's most popular drug, Bennett Alan Weinberg and Bonnie K. Bealer (2002)

The history of the coffee house starts some time near the beginning of the 16th century, when coffee houses became gathering places for the enjoyment not just of coffee, but of intellectual, cultural and social stimulation as well. The one thing that binds almost all the coffee-house histories together is the whiff of revolution and the crack of control. Their biggest crime, it seems, is their ability to give their patrons a good time.

In the earliest days of coffee-house history, the *kahwe khaneh* of Mecca provided their enthusiastic customers with coffee along with chess and other games — sometimes played for money — and also with a venue for discussions about the issues and news of the day, and for singing, dancing and musical performances. Often there were noisy arguments, and inevitably the coffee houses attracted the disapproval of the pious Mohammedans.

The coffee, served in little cups, was made from roasted beans ground to a powder and dropped into boiling water. The coffee boiler was taken off the fire several times as the liquid bubbled up to its rim. Sometimes the coffee was spiced with cinnamon and cloves; always the result was hot and powerful.

This early coffee-making was a masculine pursuit that required its own impressively decorated and packaged paraphernalia of different-sized brass pots, a heavy ladle for roasting beans over a fire, a mortar and pestle, and a set of tiny handle-less cups.

Philipe Sylvestre Dufour, a French coffee merchant, philosopher and writer, described the process of consuming the potent Arabian brew in his 17th-century book *Traitez nouveaux et curieux du café, du thé et du chocolat: ouvrage également necessaire aux medecins, et tous ceux qui aiment leur santé* (New and curious qualities of coffee, tea and chocolate: a work equally necessary for doctors, and for all who value their health):

One ought not to drink coffee, but suck it in as hot as one can. In order not to be burned, it is not necessary to place the tongue in the cup but hold the edge against the tongue with the lips above and below it, forcing it so little that the edges do not bear down, and then suck in; that is to say, swallow it sip by sip. If one is so delicate he can not stand the bitterness, he can temper it with sugar. It is a mistake to stir the coffee in the pot, the grounds being worth nothing. In the Levant it is only the scum of the people who swallow the grounds.

Whether their customers drained their cups or not, the coffee houses were corrupting the people, the Mohammedans grumbled, and surely the law of the Prophet forbidding wine must apply to this immoral brew. The rough and ready coffee houses were anathema, too, to the strict law enforcer Kha'ir Beg, who had been recently appointed governor of Mecca by the sultan of Egypt. He saw no merit in them at all and, suspicious of the enjoyment they prompted, concluded that they must be dens of vice and sedition. Intolerant of unruliness in his district, he turfed all the coffee drinkers out of the mosque and sought professional advice.

It was around 1511. Kha'ir Beg's lawyers agreed that the coffee houses in the city needed to be reformed, and called for medical advice on the humoral effects of coffee itself. The advice was mixed. One claimed that the coffee plant itself was 'cold and dry', and another that it was 'hot and dry'; others swore that the drink clouded their senses. A decision was made. Coffee was prohibited because it was intoxicating and dangerous.

All the coffee houses of Mecca were closed and their supplies of coffee, along with all the stock piled in the warehouses, were burnt. A presentment was drawn up, signed and delivered to the sultan at Cairo.

The people of Mecca, however, were decidedly unhappy with the decision and continued to drink their coffee secretly. The sultan was unimpressed too and rebuked the governor for prohibiting something that in Cairo was considered not only lawful but also enjoyable.

The law was rescinded, and again coffee flowed smoothly in the coffee houses; the singing, dancing and vigorous debates resumed, and all seemed well until 1524. Then, because of the brawling and late-night commotions of the local coffee-house clientele, the kadi of Mecca closed the coffee houses again. But this second prohibition was also short lived; the kadi's successor relicensed the *kahwe khaneh*, and coffee was poured once more.

Ten years later a preacher in Cairo, realising that the coffee houses were proving more popular than places of worship, ranted against the beverage and whipped up his congregation to such an extent that they burst from the mosque and besieged the first coffee house they came to, burning the coffee pots and dishes and attacking everyone inside. Opinion in the city was divided. The chief justice consulted the medical profession once more.

Their verdict was that drinking coffee was definitely not an act breaching the law of Mohammed and that the coffee houses should be restored. That should have been the end of it ...

Coffee house chronology

Mecca — 1500

Constantinople — 1554

Venice — 1645

Oxford — 1650

While the Bekhuis family were not rich, they were comfortable and there was enough food on the farm to keep them from hunger. But others in the Netherlands would soon be starving. The world was at war.

At Albergen, tucked against the German border, it was a time of great caution and fear. Border patrols would shoot at anything moving after the 6 p.m. curfew. Planes were shot down. Soldiers searched neighbourhoods and took furs, copper, radios, blankets and bicycles and any other means of transport. Jewish people who had not been rounded up in the house searches and loaded onto trucks were hidden in the neighbours' gardens or in the fields. Sometimes Suzy had to deliver food to them, passing it through a small, barely discernible opening in the ground. Too young to know whose land it was and unable to understand German, she was considered to be as safe as possible if she was ever stopped and questioned.

Food coupons were introduced in 1943 and brought work for the Bekhuis family. The children were dispatched each day after school to collect the colour-coded coupons from families in the district and sign their stamp books as proof of purchase. Hendrikus would then buy the goods from the wholesale markets by exchanging the coupons. The families would present their books to him and collect their food. It was complicated, time-consuming and important work. Each child had a district to collect from, and the deep snow of the bitter winters was no excuse for delay.

It was Suzy's first taste of dealing with real customers

and she loved it. Quick with figures and well organised, she carried out her duties with efficiency.

At first, Hendrikus had been able to continue selling the produce from the farm to customers who came to the house in search of food. But there came a point where he couldn't sell any more. The little he could force from the land with the limited resources available was needed now for his family. Already traumatised by the war, with the cities bombed and the country's economy destroyed, the Dutch people would discover there was more to come. The 1944–45 'Hunger Winter' bit hard.

Desperate people appeared in Overijssel, coming from further and further away in a frantic search for food as rationing tightened on the cities. Whole families had been forced to survive on tulip bulbs, sugar beet, grass, grain or whatever they could barter or scavenge, and gaunt-faced, thin skeletons of people struggled into the area in search of food. Suzy's abiding memory of the war in her village is the sight of people stumbling on the roads, collapsing and dying on the roadside from hunger. During that horrifying time 18,000 Dutch civilians died of starvation.

When the Canadian troops finally arrived to free the village in 1945, everyone ran to greet the 'beautiful' tanks. The soldiers, who had butter, corned beef and white bread, also had baskets full of chocolate and distributed it liberally. The next day the Bekhuis children, who hadn't seen sugar for years, were violently sick.

Many years later, and despite her affection for her adopted home and her respect for New Zealanders, Suzy decided that because most of them had never shared the agony of living in an occupied land, they could never fully understand her or her culture. The war was embedded in her. If she would ever marry at all, she decided, she would have to find a suitable Dutchman.

War babies, Hermanus (Herman) Bernadus and Antonius (Tony) Bernardus were born in 1940 and 1942. A little unnamed boy arrived next but died when a day old before twins Theresia (Trees) and Franciscus were born in 1945. Then disaster struck the Bekhuis family and their lives began to unravel.

In February 1945, baby Franciscus, although generally healthy, appeared to have a problem with an ear and was taken to hospital for what the family believed was a minor procedure. He never came home. Later, it became clear that he also had a weakness in his heart and his little body couldn't survive the operation. He was six weeks old.

Catharina took the death of her baby hard. She had been unwell for some time and the birth of the twins had left her severely weakened. The busy household with 13 active children and the intermittent presence of bustling housekeeping help provided by the local council was proving too much for her. To give her some relief and to ensure that she didn't have to go to hospital, Hendrikus had built her a *prieel*, or summerhouse, in the large ornamental garden where she could rest. A nurse was engaged to care for her.

The children could be with their mother for an hour at a time to talk to her as she lay there quietly and, at times, to comfort her as she wept. They felt privileged to visit her. She had a gentle nature and never spoke harshly to them or raised her hand. She was passionate about music and often listened to opera and classical music on the radio, and when she had been stronger she had played the harp. She was well dressed and always well groomed and her children recall her beautiful hair which she wore in a French roll. Going to the summer-house each day, Suzy remembers, was like visiting the queen.

Suzy had turned six on 2 September 1944 but because the school year had already just begun she was held back for almost 12 months until she could enrol. No protests or tears of exasperation from a little girl who wanted to get on with her life would make any difference. Rules were rules.

She was an observant child and sensitive to the tensions in the house, and because she was not yet at school, had plenty of time to watch and listen. One day, she was sitting at one end of the kitchen with her mother who was breastfeeding Trees. Suzy was stroking the baby's plump arms when an argument broke out without warning between her parents. Hendrikus, who was putting on his boots, threw them to the floor in a rage.

Alarmed and instantly defensive of her mother, Suzy shook a small, accusing finger at her father. 'Don't you ever do that again.'

It was a brave move for a six-year-old and one that would stand Suzy in good stead. Hendrikus had a quick temper and with the worry of a sick wife and the responsibility for a large and growing family, he could react violently. It was the children — particularly the boys — who often received a beating. Suzy, however, was rapidly learning to look after herself.

Hendrikus worked hard and expected his children to work on the land too. The Albergen farm was less than five hectares, but Hendrikus leased more land elsewhere in the district. He grew corn, oats, potatoes and a mix of vegetables, which he sold in the town from a vegetable wagon drawn by two horses. The family milked five Friesian cows and had three henhouses with 2,000 white leghorn laying hens, a large brood-house for hatching eggs, a few pigs and a small orchard.

Above: Hendrikus and Trees survey part of their large flock of white leghorn hens.The Bekhuis family also milked a few cows, raised pigs and grew vegetables on the family's small farm in Albergen.

It was dirty and never-ending labour on the farm and the children were expected to pull their weight. From the age of four, Suzy had followed her potato-gathering older brothers, picking up the *krieltjes*, the small valuable potatoes, while they harvested the larger ones. She was quick and determined, scrabbling in the dirt in her dress and clogs, and calling out every time she had her heavy bucket quarter-filled for her brothers to empty into a linen sack.

With her mother unwell, some of the household duties and the gardening fell on the oldest daughter Annie. The other children spent their out-of-school hours in the fields.

As Catharina gathered strength she began to venture out again to the markets — sometimes with Suzy on the back of her prized Raleigh bicycle — to buy small things the family needed, and buttons and thread to keep up with the endless piles of mending. For Suzy it meant welcome exposure to a world beyond the farm, and she grew to appreciate the benefits of her year held back from school. If she was good, she could go with her father on his business rounds and to the 'real' market where Hendrikus was drawn to the excitement and daring of the property auctions.

House auctions in the Netherlands are complex and follow a two-part sequence. Hendrikus would take part in the *inzet*, the first part of an auction, where starting from a low price, bid follows increasing bid until all but one bidder has dropped out. Suzy was only a young child but she knew what was going on and watched with interest.

Hendrikus, often as not, set the highest bid. The next stage was the *afslag* where the auctioneer began again from an inflated price and worked backwards toward the original set price. Tension was high. Anybody could call *mijn* and halt the bidding at any point in the auction. As long as that point was above the original highest bid, the bidder won the property and Hendrikus would win a percentage of the difference because he had set the original price.

On winning days he would leave for home with a broad smile. Sometimes, if things were not going to plan, he would end up with the property that failed to reach a higher bid. In that case, he would sell on to the next highest bidder and swallow his loss. Next time, he would do better.

The bids were fast; the atmosphere was tense. The whole noisy event was thrilling and daring, and Suzy was impressed. She loved the cut and thrust and the chance to make money. Business, she decided was far more appealing than the perpetual drudgery of a farm.

An Ottoman romance

Having their floors spread with mats, and illuminated at night by a multitude of lamps. Being the only theatres for the exercise of the profane eloquence, poor scholars attend here to amuse the people. Select portions are read, e.g. the adventures of Rustan Sal, a Persian hero. Some aspire to the praise of invention, and compose tales and fables. They walk up and down as they recite, or assuming oratorical consequence, harangue upon subjects chosen by themselves.
In one coffee house in Damascus an orator was regularly hired to tell histories at a fixed hour; in other cases he was more directly dependent upon the taste of his hearers, as at the conclusion of his discourse, whether it had consisted of literary topics or of loose and idle tales, he looked to the audience for a voluntary contribution.
At Aleppo, again, there was a man with a soul above the common, who, being a person of distinction, and one that studied merely for his own pleasure, had yet gone the round of all the coffee houses in the city to pronounce moral harangues.

Description of Arabia, Carsten Niebuhr (1774)

By the middle of the 16th century coffee houses had been established in every major city in Islam.

Although the drink of coffee had been known in Constantinople since 1517 it was not until 1554 that coffee houses were introduced to the city independently by two Syrian businessmen — Shams, who was from Damascus, and Hakam, who was from Aleppo. Shams and Hakam's respective coffee houses were seductive institutions designed for comfort and free discussion. For the price of a coffee, customers could relax on sofas and chew the fat.

The Turks loved their new coffee houses, which rapidly grew in number and increased in variety from tiny, busy coffee booths in the business districts to the richly carpeted and opulent lounges frequented by businessmen, merchants, travellers, academics, ambitious civil servants and officers of the seraglio seeking coffee, entertainment and debate.

They loved their coffee too. French scholar Antoine Galland, the first European translator of *The Arabian Nights*, wrote in *Lettre sur l'Origine et le Progres du Café* in 1699 that rich or poor, every Turk, Jew, Greek or Armenian in Constantinople drank coffee at least twice a day. Twenty coffees a day, per person, he reported, was not an uncommon average at a time when a man's refusal or neglect to provide coffee for his wife was a legitimate cause for divorce.

While they might be popular, the coffee houses seemed locked in to a never-ending conflict with the wowsers of the 16th century, and in about 1570 the imams and dervishes mounted another attack. The mosques of

Constantinople were practically empty; the coffee houses were full. This time the argument hung on the premise that as Mohammed had not known about coffee and therefore had not drunk it, his followers must not drink it either and coffee must be banned. A second potentially incriminating aspect lay in its preparation. Coffee, the religious fanatics argued, was burned and ground to charcoal, which was noted in the Koran as unsanitary.

The current mufti was decidedly coffee-unfriendly, and again coffee was forbidden by law. The people sighed loudly and continued buying their coffee from the back rooms of shops until a new coffee-drinking mufti lifted the ban and the coffee houses were restored.

Still, the coffee houses were far from safe. More than 60 years later the coffee house persecution was revived. Vizier Mahomet Kolpili, in a wholesale gesture against potential lubricants of sedition, banned coffee, tobacco and opium and, claiming that they were fire hazards, ordered the coffee houses to be burned to the ground. Kolpili meant business. For a first violation of the ban a coffee house proprietor or his customer was severely beaten; for a second infringement each was to be sewn into a leather bag and thrown into the Bosphorus.

And still the people of Constantinople covertly drank their dark brews. Time passed. The coffee houses morphed into 'coffee stalls' in market places, where the drink was boiled in large copper vessels over fires, or 'coffee bars' inside existing shops, and eventually, when Kolpili felt less threatened by coffee house politics, the regulations were relaxed.

Coffee houses, it seemed, were here to stay.

Above: Suzy, Betsy and Jan are among the many pupils assembled outside St Aloysius School for a group picture c 1947.

In September 1945 Suzy enrolled at St Aloysius, a Roman Catholic co-educational school. She might have been at school at last, but she was far from happy. The other children in her class were almost a year younger and seemed so immature. And lessons just added to the day's hard work.

Early each morning — before breakfast, church and school — it was her job to peel the potatoes for the midday meal for the family and the seasonal workers. Squatting on a three-legged stool in the *deel*, among the murmurings and smells of the cows on one side and the horses on the other, she carefully peeled what seemed like a mountain of potatoes, saving the thin peelings for her father's inspection. In the winter the pot belly stove and the breath of the animals warmed her; in the spring the breezes renewed the air. She grew to enjoy her solitude, the company of the patient animals, and her isolation from the bustle and tensions inside the house.

Breakfast was porridge and milk ladled out by Hendrikus at one of the two dining tables in the large kitchen. Then it was off to school hand-in-hand with her best friend, and nearest sister, Betsy. Home again at lunchtime, more school, a hurried snack of a sandwich or soup that had been simmering on the stove, a quick change into old clothes and back again to the land until it was almost dark and time for supper then bed.

There were the potatoes to be picked up, fresh beans and berries to be harvested, fruit to be gathered in summer and spring. When the weather was snowy or wet, there were always dried red beans to be shucked from their pods, walnuts to be cracked and vegetables to be packed. Every child had an additional regular job feeding the animals, milking the cows or caring for the house or yards. For two hours on Sundays they were allowed to play — preferably with other Catholic children.

They were well-loved children, well-dressed and never hungry, and the Bekhuis family were respected by their neighbours. They lived in a large and comfortable house in the fields of one of the most beautiful parts of the Netherlands. As an adult, Suzy looks back on them as good days, but to the young Suzy at the time it seemed there was always work, work and more work to be done.

In 1947, when it appeared that Catharina had regained some of her strength, she was diagnosed with a double hernia and told that she needed to have an operation. Only a few days before, she had cycled to see her sister Suze and had cycled home again. The family were relieved to see her looking so well.

On 29 May she was admitted to hospital. That night, after her operation, she rang the bell for assistance but nobody came to her aid. She was now bleeding heavily.

The next day was a Friday and the Bekhuis family were all busy working on the farm. Catharina was expected to come home in a day or two, and the children had been talking about her homecoming. But for now, as it was springtime, there were many tasks to be done and they expected to be well occupied for the day.

The sound of emergency sirens caused them to stop and look up from their work. Several ambulances sped into the yard and braked to a halt. 'Come quick,' said a driver, 'your mother's dying.'

There was no time to change clothes or wash. Hendrikus, grey-faced and shocked, herded his shaking children into the waiting ambulances that raced them the 15 kilometres to the hospital. They filed through the doors frightened and confused. Little Tony was shaking uncontrollably. A doctor gave them their instructions; the children were to visit their mother one at a time. They could give her a soft and gentle hug and say goodbye, and Catharina, he said, would advise them on their futures.

Trembling, the Bekhuis children entered their mother's unfamiliar room one by one. Catharina looked just like Mama. She wasn't sitting up in bed, but she didn't look like she was dying either. The doctor had insisted, however, that they would never see her again. Suzy was distraught. She grasped her mother's hand as if she would never let go.

Catharina spoke clearly without tears. Suzy had always been good at working on the land and peeling the potatoes, she told the shivering little girl. Because she was always such a well organised worker, she would like her daughter to study and become a schoolteacher or a nurse.

'No,' said Suzy through her tears. 'I don't want to be a school teacher. I want to be a businesswoman. I want to work for myself.'

Catharina Bekhuis died a few hours after her family had assembled at her bedside.

Her tragic death was totally unexpected, and despair sliced deep into her young family. Although she had been sick and had withdrawn from the busier parts of everyday family life for some time, she had always maintained a quiet and calm influence. That comforting presence was now gone.

When their mother died, Henny, the oldest child, was 20 years old. Annie, who would be 17 the following month and had become increasingly responsible for much of the household duties, would take on more of her mother's role and nurture the youngest children. It was Annie who remembered the birthdays, Annie who kept the vaccinations up to date, and Annie who dispensed sympathy. Willy was due to take up army service in the next week. Each child, in separate and lifelong ways, would have to cope with the enormous sadness and desolation of losing a mother so early. It would be 60 years before Suzy could bring herself to visit her mother's grave.

It was a devastated family then that gathered for Catharina's church service and they sobbed inconsolably. Suzy was unable to even glance in her mother's coffin. The Bruinsma family, most of whom lived in Limberg, travelled to Albergen to join them for the funeral. Theirs was a large family too, and it had been a long way to come. About 60 family members squeezed into the Bekhuis house and slept on the floor or wherever they could find a space.

The Bekhuis children barely knew the newcomers. They had vague memories of the senior Bruinsmas arriving in horse-drawn buggies and wearing traditional Dutch dress, and they remembered being required to sit quietly and respectfully throughout the occasional visits. They recalled Aunty Jo who wore an old fashioned cap and spoke Friesian with their mother, and they knew stylish Aunty Suze and her husband, Bertus, who had always visited once or twice a year on leave from Indonesia. But their coal-mining uncles and the uncles' families were virtually strangers to them.

It was good of them to come, and the Bekhuis family appreciated their support, but their gesture had a hidden and deadly barb. Unknown to both families, one of the Bruinsmas was a TB carrier.

Tuberculosis, that scourge of history, had been rife in Europe during the war. Several hundred thousand people had died; an estimated 5–10 million people had suffered from the disease. Many more were infected without knowing.

Several of the Bekhuis children contracted mild cases of the illness. Four and a half year-old Tony and Sieny aged 11, however, suffered very badly. It was an inexplicably cruel blow to a family already suffering and vulnerable. Once again ambulances pulled up in the Bekhuis yard. Tony was treated in one hospital, and Sieny, more seriously affected, was sent to a sanatorium by the sea. It was a long haul for the family to travel by train and bus to visit Sieny, and for years her brothers and sisters saw her only once or twice a year.

Again, the family had been shaken to the core. Eight year-old Suzy reacted with disbelief. If there truly was a god, how could he let her mother die? From that moment, she decided, she could no longer believe as a Catholic.

London — 1652

The Hague — 1664

Marseilles — 1671

Hamburg — 1679

Triumphant Venice

Venice's vicinity to Turkey has ... made them contract some similarity of manners; for what, except being imbued with Turkish notions, can account for the people's rage here, young and old, rich and poor, to pour down such quantities of coffee? I have already had seven cups today, and feel frightened lest we should some of us be killed with so strange an abuse of it. On the opposite shore, across the Adriatic, opium is taken to counteract its effects; but these dear Venetians have no notion of sleep being necessary to their existence ... as some or other of them seem constantly in motion, and there is really no hour of the four-and-twenty in which the town seems perfectly still and quiet.

Glimpses of Italian Society, Hester Piozzi, (1892)

The intriguing news of the coffee houses reached Europe when the Venetian traders brought coffee back from the Levant around 1615, and the Italians were charmed at once by their new find.

But, as always, coffee had to run the gauntlet of official opprobrium. Pope Clement VIII was petitioned by his priests to have it banned, claiming it was Satan's substitute for the Christian Holy Communion wine and suited only to Muslims. The pope, however, who tried the drink and liked what he tasted, gave it his blessing.

At first coffee was sold along with other drinks by

Venetian lemonade vendors, and by 1645 it was in general use throughout the country. The first Italian coffee house is said to have opened in Venice the same year.

One of the most famous of the Venetian coffee houses was Caffè Florian which was run by Floriano Francesconi under the arcades of the Procuratie Nuove in St Mark's Square and began serving coffee on 29 December 1720. It was first called 'Venezia Trionfante' or 'Triumphant Venice' but became known by its fond patrons as 'Florian's'. From a simply furnished two-room establishment it grew to become the home of Esposizione Internazionale d'Arte Contemporanea (International Exhibition of Contemporary Art), which later became known as the Venice Biennale, and it remains an elegant and opulent coffee house.

English bibliographer William Carew Hazlitt wrote in *The Venetian Republic* (1905) that 18th century Venetian coffee 'was said to surpass all others' and that Florian's was the best in Venice:

In later days, the Caffè Florian was under the superintendence of a female chef, and the waitresses used, in the case of certain visitors, to fasten a flower in the button-hole, perhaps allusively to the name. In the Piazza itself girls would do the same thing. A good deal of hospitality is, and has ever been, dispensed at Venice in the cafés and restaurants, which do service for the domestic hearth.

There were many other establishments devoted, more especially in the latest period of Venetian independence, to the requirements of those who desired such resorts for purposes of conversation and gossip. These houses were frequented by various classes of patrons — the patrician, the politician, the soldier, the artist, the old and the young. All had their special haunts where the company and the tariff were in accordance with the guests. The upper circles of male society — all above the actually poor — gravitated hither to a man.

For the Venetian of all ranks the coffee house was almost the last place visited on departure from the city, and the first visited on his return. His domicile was the residence of his wife and the repository of his possessions; but only on exceptional occasions was it the scene of domestic hospitality, and rare were the instances when the husband and the wife might be seen abroad together, and when the former would invite the lady to enter a café or a confectioner's shop to partake of an ice.

At home in Albergen, local officialdom stepped in again to provide practical help with cooking, ironing and general housework for the motherless family. Housekeepers — mostly volunteer women and largely unknown to the children — came and went from the house. Meals were mysteriously prepared. Beds were made when they were at school, and clothes cleaned and folded. One woman who seemed to be there all the time was devoted to an endless production line of washing that she hung up to dry flapping on the vast clotheslines strung up in the yards.

Suzy was now in her second year at school, and things were looking up. By good fortune she was now in the same class as twins Jan and Betsy, and they drew strength from each other. School was proving to be fun as well. Suzy was a good high-jumper, a fast runner and, with her long arms and legs, an effective goalkeeper at soccer.

With his children rapidly growing up — and the oldest ones now leaving school — Hendrikus looked beyond the farm as the primary means to support them. The answer to keeping the large family together and providing them with employment, it seemed, was to establish a business. Land was scarce, building resources were stretched and rules were strict.

The Netherlands had been traumatised by the war. Although the end to the fighting had suggested the country might recover quickly, it had not proved to be the case. The rationing continued for years, and there was high unemployment, a claustrophobic population density and the highest birth rate in Europe. When the Dutch had finally conceded Indonesian sovereignty in 1949, thousands of troops had returned from Indonesia along with about 250,000 Dutch nationals who had been ordered home too. The Netherlands was full to bursting.

Hendrikus, however, had his eye on the former policeman's house in the nearby town of Almelo, about 10 kilometres from the farm, which had a large garden and a yard suitable for the construction of a shop. He wrote to the authorities, explaining his circumstances. With the serious shortage of buildings and land it was a long shot, but worth a try. To his relief, he received a positive reply. His large family could establish a business in Almelo.

Hendrikus continued to sell his potatoes, vegetables and fruit door to door from his horse and carriage. It was a popular service because he allowed the housewives to taste the fruit before they bought any. He opened a shop in the barn behind the house and installed Sieny, when she was well enough, behind the counter, and customers flocked to the cosy barn for produce and gossip. The Bekhuis family now had a house and farm in Albergen, which would still provide produce for the markets, and a house and a greengrocery store in the town of Almelo.

The greengrocery was very successful, and Hendrikus built a new and up-to-date shop. The building it occupied was fairly large, and the shop was square in plan. One wall displayed liqueurs, wine, and unusual and exotic fruits. Another stored the vegetables and more ordinary fruit. There was ice cream for sale too, and big, modern machines for peeling potatoes or slicing cabbages and other vegetables at the customers' requests.

Sieny ran the shop along with two employees from the town. Henny and Gerard, who had also left school, each operated a horse-drawn cart selling fruit and vegetables to their own clientele. Willy worked first for a farmer in Tubbergen, then later in a coal mine in Limberg. Toos remained on the farm and Marietje worked for a family in Almelo. Suzy, Betsy, Jan, Herman, Tony and Trees were still at school.

Annie continued to look after the household and the family, doing the cooking and gardening. 'You'd better marry quick,' Suzy told her older sister, 'because you're so old, you'll die soon.' It became a perennial family joke.

Hendrikus remained the overseer of all.

Next page: The Bekhuis' greengrocery in Almelo was busy and successful and provided much needed income and employment for the family. Suzy and two helpers are pictured behind the counter.

Mars
SPRITS

Zuurkool
DE NEDERLANDEN

Suzy was now at Mulo High School and champing at the bit. Soon it would be her chance to leave and go to work.

But there was another challenge to face before she left high school. At St Aloysius school she had suffered from a bad case of head lice. It wasn't unusual for the times — most of Europe seemed to be afflicted — and the family doctor assured Hendrikus it had nothing to do with hygiene within the household. It was highly contagious, so it was simply bad luck.

For Suzy, however, the situation was supremely embarrassing. A self-confessed 'fuss-pot' about how she looked at all times, she was mortified by this. Appearances mattered. As an eight-year-old she had rebelled against the design of the waistband on her first communion dress, resulting in a tearful family drama and a new design. She not only had head lice, but also an accompanying case of ugly and painful boils.

At high school she was unlucky to have head lice a second time. To protect the rest of the students, and until the medical treatment took effect, she was required to sit at the front of the class. The whole situation was unbearably humiliating. The moment she turned 16, she announced, she was leaving school.

Her determination was founded on much more than a severe knock to teenage pride. For the two years she had attended high school Suzy had been making plans to set up her own business.

Above: Eight year-old Suzy poses in her modified communion dress.

Her last pre-school year she had spent largely with her father as he had gone about his business, and her experience collecting coupons had sometimes taken her into the poorer, predominantly Catholic, eastern suburbs of Twente and exposed her to the sounds and scenes of domestic violence. The size of the families — which, she believed, were pressed by the Church to produce a baby a year regardless of their ability to support them — had disturbed her. So too had the family's insistence on buying their meat from the Catholic butcher, whose shop was much further away than the Protestant equivalent. None of it made sense.

She had queried her father on the topic.

'You know my girlfriend? Well her father's a doctor and she only has one brother and one sister, and she always has beautiful clothes and they go on holidays. Why do all these families have 10 or 12 children?'

'Well,' Hendrikus replied, 'that's just the way it is.'

There was another puzzle too. For as long as she had lived in Almelo, she had heard a neighbour heading off to work every morning at 6.30. He was a small man, he had 10 children and he wore clogs. Every morning he would clip-clop down the road over the brick-paved footpath and every evening, he clip-clopped back again. Day in; day out; summer and winter; rain or shine. Working for a boss, Suzy decided, meant hard relentless graft and working too hard led to a shortened life.

The violence, the overcrowding, the poverty and dominance of the textile factories in the area were good enough incentives to resist marriage and to always be independent, Suzy concluded. She intended to live long and live well. As soon as she could she would leave the town and make her own way in the world.

Suzy turned 16 in 1954, and Hendrikus agreed she could leave school.

'Right, madam,' he said. 'From today you work and you pay board.'

She was outfitted with a box tied by string around her neck and displaying six different types of potatoes. It was her task to go door-knocking and persuade potential customers to choose their preferred potato types and buy them in 25-kilogram bags. Each day, Hendrikus told her, she would receive 25 per cent of the profit she made. Once she had 10 bags on order, she could hire a bicycle with large buckets attached to carry the bags.

So she did.

She sold her 10 bags, hired the bicycle, sold more bags, returned the hired bicycle and bought her own. Sometimes she sold 50 bags in a day and delivered them all. The bicycle was superseded by a motorised cycle and trailer for more vegetables, and the local newspaper took her photograph and interviewed her. She was in business.

She bought a Volkswagen Kombi, diversified into a wider range of vegetables and by the time she was 20 years old, she was driving a truck and buying produce at the markets for her own customers, and for her two brothers and father as well.

Right: Suzy's first business venture was in 1954 selling potatoes from door to door with a display box tied around her neck.

66

Being in business was every bit as good as she had imagined. It seemed to be coded in her bones. She loved driving the truck to the market — in Deventer or Utrecht or wherever the produce or the prices seemed best — three times a week, even five times if business was brisk. One day she was stopped by the police. She had a heavy load on the truck and they wanted to check it. They asked for her licence and with relief she handed it over. She had been driving the truck to the markets for about a year; her licence was one month old.

She had to be at the markets early so she set off from home at about 5 a.m. The huge hangars were full of activity at that hour. Men rubbing their fingers to keep off the cold and blowing conversation bubbles of steam noisily stacked truckloads of boxes in auction lots or cast experienced eyes over the rows and rows of produce.

Suzy strode long-legged up and down the aisles carefully inspecting the crates. A no-nonsense, slim young woman in trousers she was competing in an essentially man's world. She neatly marked off in her booklet what it was she wanted for her own clients and those of her brothers and father. The markets received vegetables and fruit sent from all over Europe, thousands and thousands of crates of potatoes and cabbages and cauliflowers of varying sizes and quality. It took about an hour to complete the rounds and fill out her preferred purchases before the auction.

Above: Following her initial success selling potatoes, Suzy bought a motorised cycle and trailer for selling a range of vegetables. The local newspaper interviewed her and published this photograph.

Sitting in rows at a desk again was like school — only much, much better. She was now part of a Dutch horticultural tradition that had begun 70 years before, and like all the men around her, she had her eyes fixed on the big auction clock.

A Dutch price clock starts at what is recognised as a high price for the produce on sale. The hand on the clock points to the top, at the beginning price, then the hand moves anti-clockwise to decreasing prices and the bidding begins. You have to be quick to press the button to register your bid and you have to be sure of what you are doing. There is no reneging. Once that initial bid is made, the first deal is done and the price is 'set'.

If she really needed that particular batch of spinach or cherries, Suzy might pay a little too much for it, but she got what she wanted. There was always the chance she could make up the difference on the crates of cabbages. It was a challenge; it was a gamble. It was fast and exciting, and Suzy had been well trained by watching her father bid for the houses.

The men liked this tall, blonde, young woman who was proving to be extremely canny and determined to strike the best deal. Most of them recognised her as part of the Bekhuis family and knew she had lost her mother when she was a child. They respected her independence and her rapidly growing skills, and they were kind to her. She thrived on being part of their community. Her young friends in the cafés back in Almelo weren't as impressed though. 'So you set the price for Europe for cauliflowers? Oh yeah. So what?'

But their lack of interest didn't faze Suzy. At last she was making her way in the adult world of trading. She was on her way.

She began to expand her business, employing 15- and 16-year-olds to weigh, sort and deliver the vegetables after school. If they were worth it, she paid her workers four guilders an hour rather than the three her father and brothers offered. That way, she discovered, she secured the best quality staff and they stayed the longest.

Her franchise was now taking a larger percentage of the profits. At nights, Hendrikus, Henny, Gerard and Suzy would sit at one of the big dining tables and count the money they had made, sort out the shop wages and share out the profits. Suzy would hand back to Hendrikus part of her share to pay for her board.

But life wasn't just about work. Now that she was earning her own money, Suzy could spend it the way she wanted and clothes were at the top of the list. She liked good clothes and was prepared to pay for them. When she saw what she wanted in a shop — a gold-embroidered velvet skirt; a black Italian blouse — she would ask for it to be put aside, then look at the price and finally make sure she earned enough to pay for it during the following month. Hendrikus, who never approved of time payment, never knew. When his rapidly growing daughter dyed her hair blonde, however, he did notice and he was angry.

'Oh, I spent too much time in the sun,' Suzy told him airily.

She liked cars and motor bikes too. She rode her father's old Harley Davison motorbike secretly, when he was having a Sunday afternoon nap, switching it off well before she came home, cruising the last distance silently and carefully parking it in the same way back in the shed.

Every year on Whit Monday a motorcycle race was organised in nearby Tubbergen. The race course included Almelo, and people would gather at the sides of the road to watch the spectacle. Suzy sensed a business opportunity. She loaded a truck with empty orange crates and drove them to the race circuit. For a few guilders each, she rented the orange crate 'seats' to the spectators for the day, gathered the crates at the end of the race and took them home again.

She might be doing well at work, Hendrikus warned, but there was still much to learn.

'You're too high in your head. You're too high up there. Come down because you might end up in the gutter,' he told her.

'Pooh! I'm not going to slave.'

Sometimes Suzy helped out in the shop and one day, short of cash, she borrowed coins from the till. Hendrikus caught her. Suzy protested. It was the first time she had ever stolen anything, she told him.

But Hendrikus was unmoved. Whether it was the first time or the tenth time didn't matter. The crucial issue was that no child of his would ever steal.

He whacked her on the hands and, furious that she had let him down, ordered her to write over and over, 'I'm a thief. I'm a thief. I'm a thief.'

With hands red and stinging, she was thoroughly humiliated and never forgot her father's lesson. Business was not just about making money. It was about honesty as well.

Next page: Hendrikus pauses on his rounds selling vegetables from his truck with (from left) Suzy, Henny, Betsy and two young friends.

With two homes — one at the Albergen farm and one in Almelo — the family moved back and forth between them, each person choosing which one to sleep at according to the events of the day. Washing and ironing were done by Toos at the farm. On Saturdays at noon, family and friends in Almelo would have lunch cooked by Sieny — bacon, potatoes and vegetables with lashings of gravy. Meat was still scarce so lunch at the Bekhuis house was considered a treat.

While the farm and the business were both running successfully, life at home was not always as smooth. Hendrikus continued to be volatile, sometimes challenging his rapidly maturing sons and his daughters often without reason and too frequently with violence. Suzy, however, stood her ground. One day when she was 18 and out on the farm, her father asked her to do something for him. She was in a hurry. She had other things to do and the task went undone. When she arrived back home, Hendrikus caught her by surprise and struck her. She stood firm. 'You do that to me again and I'll go to the police,' she told him.

Undoubtedly lonely and quite possibly bewildered by the responsibilities of so many mouths to feed and lives to shape, Hendrikus had made some attempts to marry again. After church services on Sunday mornings it was customary in Almelo to adjourn to a café or restaurant for coffee and perhaps a liqueur. Perhaps it was here that he met prospective wives and mothers for his large brood. Maybe he took them out at night for a drink, a meal or just an adult conversation, but the children tucked up safely and asleep didn't know. Several times he brought one or the other of the women home for coffee and family inspection. After she had gone, the family got down to business around the dining tables. Was she suitable, Hendrikus asked? 'No, we don't like her. Don't bring her back,' was the reply. So he didn't.

One after the other, the women stopped visiting.

Suzy was happy to push the boundaries for herself. All her life she had wanted to be number one within the family and at school — in everything except lessons. Everybody told her she took after her father, resembling him in both looks and drive. Her high principles came from her Bruinsma genes. The attention-seeking part of her, they said, came from her namesake, Aunty Suze.

She had always had definite ideas about what she would and would not wear. Aunty Suze had introduced her as a little girl to the delights of beautiful silks, well-cut clothes and shiny accessories from Indonesia. Catharina had a seamstress make new clothes for Suzy and her sisters from Suze's cast-offs. As a young woman Suzy recognised quality in clothing and resolved that she would always have plenty of it. She was an outgoing young woman and spoke and acted without malice but sometimes before she had thought things through and her ingenuousness could get her into trouble. She offended her sister deeply when she spontaneously kissed Marietje's new boyfriend on his first visit to the farm. She had known him vaguely for some time and they were on friendly greeting terms. She was pleased to see him and showed it, but earned a face slapping from her furious sister.

She wasn't above arguing fiercely with her brothers, either, and still bears a scar where, in frustration and retaliation, one once threw a knife back at her.

At 20 years old she was beginning to resent the restrictions Hendrikus continued to impose on her life. She was becoming financially independent, smoked constantly, dressed well and longed for a life of sophistication. One night she 'borrowed' her father's shiny, black Opel Kapitän and drove with her girlfriends over the border to visit a German nightclub. There was no fear of them drinking as all of them preferred to nurse a shandy or a Coca-Cola for an entire night. Instead, they were looking for bright lights and fun. Suzy didn't arrive back at the farm until one the next morning. The curfew for the entire Bekhuis family, regardless of age, was 11 p.m.. She had it all thought through. Hendrikus was in bed asleep and she knew that if she switched off the car's engine and the lights, she could cruise silently up the drive and round behind the barn and park it exactly as he had left it. No-one would be any wiser.

Right: Suzy received this driver's licence when she was 20 years old and after she had been driving confidently for some time.

NAAM Bekhuis

(voor gehuwde vrouw of weduwe naam echtgenoot en eigen naam)

VOORNAMEN Susanna H.

(eerste voluit)

PLAATS EN DATUM VAN GEBOORTE Tubbergen 2-9-193[illegible]

ADRES [illegible]

TE Almelo

Handtekening van de houder:

S. Bekhuis

AFGEGEVEN DOOR

DE COMMISSARIS DER KONINGIN IN DE PROVINCIE OVERIJSSEL,

TE ZWOLLE, DE 21 JUL 1958

GELDIG TOT 21 JUL 1963

No 0001

All went to plan and she crept into the house. But she hadn't reckoned on Henny, who was waiting up for her, sleepless with anxiety that his father would discover her deception and terrified that she had had an accident. Hugely relieved and angry all in one, her normally gentle oldest brother struck her as she came into the room. She retaliated with her fists and chipped his front tooth. Both brother and sister were remorseful; both were shocked at what they had done and kept it to themselves.

Suzy is undeniably attractive, with a statuesque beauty that makes heads turn. As a young woman she had many friends — including boyfriends. There was one for walking with in the park, another for accompanying her to the cinema, another one was suitable for going dancing with and yet another for generally going out. She liked them all and slept with none of them.

With no mother to confide in and petrified of the consequences of intimacy, she had once confessed to her father that she had French-kissed a boy. Would she be pregnant? She was still not interested in having sex. Sex meant children — too many children. Too many children meant being trapped. Besides, she reasoned, the boyfriends she had so far weren't shaping up to be marriageable.

One who was from a wealthy family once asked her over to his home for coffee. She was reluctant. 'Ah well,' he said, 'if the garage won't come to the house, the house will have to come to the garage.' Suzy was furious. He was from a rich family, so he was the house. He saw her as only 'the garage'. That was it.

Being 'up oneself' has always been anathema to Suzy. Respect, she believes, is not something one inherits. It is something that one earns — usually as the result of some very hard work.

Above: With a successful business and a steady income, Suzy enjoyed buying good clothes and going on outings. Here, she and her sisters Marietje and Sieny are pictured outside a favourite restaurant in Denekamp.

A victory for free speech

*ENTER, Sirs, freely, but first, if you please,
Peruse our civil orders, which are these.
First, gentry, tradesmen, all are welcome hither,
And may without affront sit down together:
Pre-eminence of place none here should mind,
But take the next fit seat that he can find:
Nor need any, if finer persons come,
Rise up for to assign to them his room;
To limit men's expense, we think not fair,
But let him forfeit twelve-pence that shall swear.
He that shall any quarrel here begin,
Shall give each man a dish t'atone the sin;
And so shall he, whose compliments extend
So far to drink in coffee to his friend;
Let noise of loud disputes be quite forborne,
Nor maudlin lovers here in corners mourn,
But all be brisk and talk, but not too much;
On sacred things, let none presume to touch
Nor profane Scripture, nor saucily wrong
Affairs of state with an irreverent tongue:
Let mirth be innocent, and each man see
That all his jests without reflection be;
To keep the house more quiet and from blame,
We banish hence cards, dice and every game;
Nor can allow of wagers, that exceed
Five shillings, which ofttimes do troubles breed;
Let all that's lost or forfeited be spent
In such good liquor as the house doth vent.*

And customers endeavour, to their powers,
For to observe still, seasonable hours.
Lastly, let each man what he calls for pay,
And so you're welcome to come every day.

Bill of regulations posted routinely in 17th century English coffee houses

The coffee houses of London are legendary. They were hotbeds of gossip and political debate, a men-only domain that dominated the city's social structure and caused the authorities no end of bother.

The English first heard of coffee in 1601 when William Parry wrote of his travels in the East and the custom of the 'damned infidels' in Aleppo of 'drinking a certain liquor, which they do call Coffe, which is made of seede much like mustard seede, which will some intoxicate the braine like our Metheglin [mead].' While the English were certainly aware of the drink and intrigued by early, and not always accurate, descriptions, it was not until 1650 that a Jew from Lebanon called Jacob or Jacobs — or Jobson according to some sources — opened the first English coffee house in Oxford. And there, coffee, Isaac D'Israeli wrote, 'was by some who delighted in noveltie, drank'.

Two years later, a Greek named Pasqua Rosée opened the first coffee house in London, which is widely attributed to be the foundation of London's social and political life of the time. Others followed enthusiastically plying their trade to a growing crowd of customers — but at a price.

Officialdom had been quick to realise the profits to be made from this new and increasingly popular commodity. The English statute books of 1660 record that the makers of coffee, along with tea and chocolate and 'other outlandish drinks', were taxed four pence for every gallon made and sold. A cup of coffee did not come cheaply.

In addition, in 1663 all English coffee houses had to be licensed at a fee of twelve pence, and any unlicensed owners were fined five pounds a month until they conformed. It was a costly business and with increased taxes on tea, coffee and newspapers, prices continued to rise. A dish of coffee in 1714 was two pence and coffee itself was retailed at five shillings per pound, just under a workman's weekly wage.

The first coffee houses of London were customarily upstairs and comprised a single large room with separate tables reserved for discussion of individual topics. The customers drank dark, strong coffee served in small saucerless dishes and tobacco pipe smoking seemed compulsory. Coffee house keepers issued their own tokens in lieu of small change, which was scarce at the time, and these original 'loyalty cards' could be redeemed at other houses within the neighbourhood.

Above all, these early coffee houses were meeting places for the lively exchange of ideas lubricated by the coffee. The entrance fee was a penny, and debate at the more refined 'penny universities' was vigorous and gossip as sharp as a rapier.

Each coffee house assumed its own character and served its own clientele, as Thomas Babington Macaulay pointed out in his *History of England* (1848, 1855):

Nobody was excluded from these places who laid down his penny at the bar. Yet every rank and profession, and every shade of religious and political opinion had its own headquarters ... There were Puritan coffee-houses where no oath was heard, and where lank-haired men discussed election and reprobation through their noses; Jew coffee-houses, where dark-eyed money changers from Venice and Amsterdam greeted each other; and Popish coffee-houses, where, as good Protestants believed, Jesuits planned over their cups another great fire, and cast silver bullets to shoot the king.

So, a good time was had by all. But, in the history of coffee houses, that could prove a tempting motive for persecution.

The first attack came from the tavern and ale-house keepers, who were unimpressed with the growing popularity of coffee and fulminated against this 'beverage from the East' in a barrage of pamphlets.

'Ninny broth' or 'Turkey gruel', the critics claimed, was a dangerous drink.

The next attack came from closer to home — in fact from home itself. In 1674 *The Women's Petition against Coffee, representing to public consideration the grand inconveniences accruing to their sex from the excessive use of the drying and enfeebling Liquor* added to a lively controversy over the advantages and disadvantages of 'the marriage of the Turk'.

Women, barred from England's coffee houses, claimed they were keeping their men away from home, and that coffee was making men as 'unfruitful as the deserts where that unhappy berry is said to be bought'. The whole of the English race, the pamphlet suggested, might be in danger of extinction.

Then the king entered the fray. Charles II, who received considerable revenue from coffee and owed his restoration in part to the coffee house's liberty of speech, was nevertheless suspicious of 'the great inconveniences arising from the great number of persons that resort to coffee-houses'. By 10 January 1676, he commanded, all licences would be revoked and coffee houses closed.

The reaction was strong and vocal, and people from all walks of life protested loudly. The coffee-house owners pointed out too that it was the king himself that would lose revenue. Then Charles backed down. Two days before the new law was to take effect, a second proclamation announced that out of his 'princely consideration and royal compassion' the coffee houses could stay open until 24 June. No further attempt to close them was made. It was a victory for free speech — and for the coffee house.

One weekend, when Suzy and her friends were sitting around relaxing and talking, the idea of emigrating took hold. Through her work selling vegetables in the streets, Suzy had a good idea of the economy in the Netherlands. Things were pretty grim throughout the country, she told her friends. There were just too many people. It would be at least 12 years before any one of them could buy a house, and there was no real future in Europe.

'Let's go and emigrate and we'll leave all this misery behind,' she suggested. She was 20 years old.

It wasn't an outrageous proposal. An 'experiment' in 1939 had transported five carefully selected young, Dutch carpenters to New Zealand, and on 26 June Wellington's *Evening Post* had announced their arrival:

DUTCH SETTLERS
ARTISANS ARRIVE TO WORK FOR GOVERNMENT
(By Telegraph – Press Association)
AUCKLAND, This Day.

The first party to arrive under what is stated to be a new immigration scheme sponsored by the Dutch and New Zealand Governments, five young Dutchmen, qualified carpenters, arrived by the Monowai *from Vancouver.*
They are leaving this afternoon for Wellington, where they will be employed on the State building projects. They are a fine type, of athletic build and well educated, and are eager to reside in New Zealand. Two are engaged to be married, and are sending later for their fiancées. Two

of them have studied English by correspondence. Their fares were partly paid by the Dutch Government under an agreement stated to have been made with the New Zealand Government providing for the immigration of a large number of Dutch setters, principally carpenters, skilled labourers, farm labourers, and domestic servants. The scheme is described in an authoritative quarter as 'important and comprehensive,' though its application will probably be gradual.

Reports are to be submitted to both Governments on the suitability of the immigrants and on the immigrants' impressions of conditions in New Zealand.
As work becomes available the quota will be increased, and a steady inflow is expected.
The men were met on the Monowai *by a Government placement officer, Mr Elsbury, and the Dutch Consul, Captain Bauer.*

It was stated from a Government source today that the five carpenters who arrived by the Monowai *had paid their own fares to New Zealand, and by arrangement with the Vice-Consul for the Netherlands, if they are not entirely satisfactory, they are to be returned to the Netherlands. The arrangement was to be regarded entirely as an experiment.*

The expected 'steady inflow' of immigrants to follow had been interrupted by the war. Now, however, the slow post-war recovery, high unemployment, the strict social controls and stifling bureaucracy of the Netherlands had increasingly brought more pressure from dissatisfied people, spawning new immigration arrangements and prompting thousands more Dutch people to seek their fortunes in other countries. A survey in 1947–48 had revealed that more than a third of the Dutch population had contemplated emigration after the war.

The Dutch government, facing all the social, environmental and economic problems that went with overcrowding, was in full agreement. It was even prepared to pay its nationals to leave and, by means of a vigorous media campaign, had been actively encouraging them to do so. Furthermore, New Zealand, Australia, Canada and South Africa, with their booming post-war economies and labour shortages, had proved to be willing recipients of young migrants from the Netherlands. The assisted passage scheme began in 1950 with 55 Dutch dairy workers flown on a direct flight to Whenuapai. Senior immigration official Dr Reuel Lochore, writing in *From Europe to New Zealand* in 1951 had made it plain that New Zealand was keen to welcome more Europeans to the New Zealand fold:

We must man the frontiers. New Zealand is a frontier land ... We must make new Britishers: by procreating and by assimilation; by making suitable aliens into vectors of the British way of life that still has so much to give to the world ... Our new Britishers should be chosen principally from the uprooted and dispossessed to whom Europe offers no home and no job ... It is our last chance of making the cousin stock of Europe into new Britishers.

In the original agreement, Wellington had asked The

Hague for 2,000 skilled immigrants. By 1971, about 20,000 Dutch people were scattered throughout New Zealand.

So Suzy's plan was hatched.

Shortly after she had left school, Suzy had realised that despite her early success in business, the haste with which she had put an end to her formal education might have been a mistake. Perhaps her mother had been right. Perhaps she should have stayed on and studied. She had thought earlier that she might like to be an accountant — the skills would certainly be useful now — so she had enrolled in a private accountancy class. Two evenings a week she went to her teacher's house and he taught her about cash registers, bookkeeping, wages and taxes.

Now she added English lessons to her weekly routine. If she was going to apply to immigrate to New Zealand — and that was certainly the latest plan — she had better learn more of the language.

There was much to be done in a year. The accountancy studies would have to go as she would need to work harder to earn the money to get a wardrobe of suitable clothes together, buy a suitcase and pay for travel to The Hague for interviews.

For the first interview there were dental checks and health checks — including X-rays for TB — to be completed, a passport to be arranged and a letter of recommendation to be written. Joop Aalders announced that he would go to New Zealand with Suzy. Others of the group of friends decided to try Canada or Australia. It was enormously exciting. There was adventure in the air.

Thankfully, the X-rays proved to be clear, and Hendrikus agreed, if reluctantly, to write Suzy a letter of recommendation as he had been her only employer:

I, the undersigned, Herr Bekhuis of Almelo, merchant in fruit and vegetables declare herewith that my daughter Susanna Maria Bekhuis, born 2 September 1938, ever since 1953 has been working for me. In the very beginning she worked only as a shop assistant making orders ready and delivering them. When she turned 18 she had a van and had her own clientele which she established along with her business by herself and without any help. I can also add that she is in possession of all the licences required for vehicles with more than two wheels.

Once she had received her driver's licence, Suzy had made a few trips with her father and Gerard to Germany, to France and to Belgium and, depending on the distance, had gone sometimes just for the day, or at other times made a holiday of it and stayed in different villages en route. She drove them in the big Opel Kapitän, one hand on the wheel, the other holding a cigarette. She had once spent a weekend in Luxembourg with her 'up-himself' boyfriend — Suzy sleeping on the top floor of the hotel and the boyfriend at the bottom. But that was the extent of her travels. Now she was about to leave everything and almost everyone she knew for an unknown country on the other side of the world.

She had a year to get everything together and then she was on her way.

Next page: Hendrikus, Gerard and Suzy pose for a holiday snap.

henfels

Counting the beans

The Dutch roast coffee properly, and make it well. The service is in individual pots, or in demi-tasses on a silver, nickel, or brass tray, and accompanied by a miniature pitcher containing just enough cream (usually whipped), a small dish about the size of an individual butter plate holding three squares of sugar, and a slender glass of water. This service is universal; the glass of water always goes with the coffee.

All About Coffee, William Ukers (1935)

The Dutch took careful note of the reports of coffee that travellers brought back to Europe. Great merchants and shrewd traders, they were experienced in dealing with the Orient and with the Venetians. If they could grow coffee in their colonies, they decided, they could make their home markets headquarters for world trade in the product and capture the market. The Dutch East India Company moved swiftly.

As early as 1614, Dutch traders were investigating the possibilities for coffee growing and trading, and two years later Pieter van dan Broeck brought the first coffee from Mocha to Holland. In 1640 in Amsterdam, a Dutch merchant named Wurffbain sold the first commercial shipment of coffee from Mocha. Driving the Portuguese out of Ceylon in 1658 gave the Dutch their first chance of cultivating the very tradeworthy bean, but it was the first Arabian seedlings sent to Java in 1696 and again in 1699 that cemented the coffee trade of the Dutch East Indies and made 'Java' coffee a household word. Cultivation and trade secure, the Dutch could now begin to enjoy the coffee house.

The first Dutch coffee house was opened in The Hague in 1664, and others soon followed in Amsterdam and Haarlem. Unlike the Scandinavians who, during the 18th century, first taxed coffee then prohibited it, then taxed it again and prohibited it several times more, the Dutch were resolute and broke the pattern of persecution.

There was no wailing about the so-called dangers of coffee houses to either Dutch health or hearth from medical or religious circles. Instead, in their constructive and practical way Dutch craftsmen turned their minds to improving the paraphernalia of coffee-making, turning out new and clever designs for coffee grinders, coffee roasters and coffee pots and thereby vastly improving the whole coffee service.

In one of the few European countries that have never moved to ban coffee, the Dutch have extended their tolerance even further to the approval of 'coffee shops' that openly sell marijuana.

Above: Suzy turned 21 before she sailed from the Netherlands to New Zealand.

Right: Suzy and Joop in the Netherlands.

The *Johan van Oldenbarnevelt* had made many trips to Australia and New Zealand. Built in 1929 for the Nederland Line, she was named after a great 16th century statesman and at the time, with seven passenger decks, a bar and swimming pool with a retractable roof, she was considered innovative and elegant. In 1941 she became a troop ship under the management of the Orient Line but still with a Dutch crew and able to carry 4,000 Allied troops. At the end of the war, she returned to the Amsterdam to Indonesia route, finally transporting Dutch troops home from Indonesia.

Withdrawn from the East Indies service in 1950 as the political climate in Indonesia changed, the *Johan van Oldenbarnevelt* was placed by the Nederland Line on the migrant service to South Africa and Australia. On 2 September 1950 she left Amsterdam on her first voyage to Australia and a new role that would last for the next 12½ years. She was known by New Zealanders as 'JVO' and Wellington adopted her. On her last trip before heading back to Europe to become a Greek cruise ship, Captain Klingen, her master at the time, in recognition of her special relationship with Wellington presented the ship's bell to Upper Hutt College.

In 1960, however, she sailed from Amsterdam on 11 April newly refurbished on a 26,112-nautical mile, round-the-world service. She was carrying 1,210 passengers ready to enjoy the newly installed nightclub, a second swimming pool with a colourful 'Lido Bar' and a new soda fountain. The passengers on board were a mix of holidaymakers on a cruise and young Dutch émigrés, including Suzy and Joop, heading to new homes. The young women's cabins were on one deck; the young men slept below. There was bingo and dancing to the Mimmo Bruno Orchestra, swimming and socialising, and along the way there would be Southampton, Genoa, Port Said, Suez, Aden, Fremantle, Melbourne, Sydney and finally Wellington to explore.

The ship arrived in Southampton the next day and most of the passengers disembarked to see the city. Except Suzy. She stayed on board quietly reading in a deckchair as all the others enthusiastically followed the tourist trails.

Above: Suzy explores Genoa, a week after leaving Amsterdam.

Her initial excitement at travelling had worn off and she was seriously traumatised. Her father's distress at leaving her had been far more severe than she ever could have imagined. For the first time in her life this seemingly confident young woman was truly alone. Her large boisterous family had been left behind, and while Joop was her good friend, she had soon realised that he would never become her lifelong partner. Joop, she decided, was destined for a life of fun — an easy life — whereas her ambitions were far more sober. Her hopes and dreams were focused entirely on running her own business.

While she was pleased to have escaped what she saw as the 'misery of Holland' she was sad too. It had always been home, and right now she was homeless.

In addition, there was the worry that while almost all activities on the ship had been paid for — except alcohol and gambling — the outings on shore were expensive and Suzy had limited financial resources to draw on. Her preparations for the trip had been costly, and as her business was simply absorbed back into the family without anything to sell, she had no capital. She was frightened and vulnerable, and beginning to doubt that she should be on this ship at all.

There were other concerns too. Without a mother from a young age and with a changing team of anonymous household help, the young Suzy had never dwelt long on the finer points of housekeeping and had never been involved in the process of washing clothes. Clean clothes were laid out daily on her bed at home and she had never paused to consider how that occurred. Now, responsible for her own welfare she had to learn. She confided in the captain's wife, who told her how to soak and wash her clothes, hang them up to dry in her cabin. Greatly relieved and grateful for the advice, Suzy complied.

When the *Johan van Oldenbarnevelt* arrived in Genoa a week after leaving Amsterdam, Suzy was persuaded to go ashore with a group of friends and an escort from the ship and have a cup of coffee. To her relief, nothing dreadful happened and she enjoyed having the Italians fuss over her white-blonde hair. By the time the ship had passed through the Suez Canal Suzy was feeling more cheerful, trying out her English with the first-class passengers and playing dominoes and deck games.

The young single women shared cabins near the first-class section, and there were strict rules about mixing with the young men. Captain Groenland, true to his word, reserved a place for Suzy at his table and, along with his wife, kept an eye on her.

At Fremantle many of the young migrants left the ship for their new homes, more disembarked at Melbourne and more at Sydney. Australians had been informed that the ship with their new citizens was about to arrive, and crowds had gathered at the docks to welcome them. They were also happy to meet the other passengers heading for New Zealand with their strange accents and unfamiliar customs, and Joop and Suzy were whisked off by friendly locals to have coffee and to be shown the sights, with the promise of a return safely in time for sailing.

When the ship docked in Wellington on 23 May 1960 it was a beautiful, misty morning and, as the first-class passengers disembarked, the young immigrants were mustered and presented to the customs officials. Suzy's first priority was to take out health insurance with the money she had set aside in her wallet — just as Hendrikus had instructed his children: 'Always keep a little money back and make sure you have insurance for your health.' He had drummed it into them all and Suzy was his most conscientious pupil. She now had £5 left with which to make her new future.

Passports were checked, fingerprints taken. Outside and way down below the ship, Suzy could see her brother Willy waiting and she grew impatient. Forty-two days at sea was a lifetime when you were only 21 and she was ready to get off and get on with her life, but there was still more to be done and still the same questions to be answered.

'Where are you going?' the official asked her.

'I have an older brother in Invercargill.'

'Well then, we think it's best for you to go to Invercargill. What would you like to do?'

"I want to be a waitress.'

'A waitress?'

'Yep.'

"Look, you can get plenty of jobs as a waitress here. Don't you want to be a nurse?'

'No. I don't want to be a nurse. I like serving people.'

The group was herded off the boat and assembled again on the wharf and instructed to stay there. This was Suzy's first footfall in her new country and she had no intention of being hobbled. She slipped away from the group and ran to the edge of the quay for a better look at Wellington. She saw the lights strung around the hills and reflecting in the dark waters of the harbour, the profiles of buildings and the shadowy hills beyond. It looked like a real city. Suzy Bekhuis from the two-storey village of Almelo was entranced. Wellington sparkled and shimmered and won her heart.

Above: In Port Said, the local children prove willing to be in the photograph of their young, blonde visitor.

Suzy is pictured in Aden with local officers (above) and with Joop (below), and footsore in Sydney (right).

Staying On

This was it then, the new country, the fresh start.

Suzy's New Zealand family gathered around her, and all her apprehension, her shyness and fear just melted away. There was Willy and his new wife June come all the way from Invercargill, and Jan, who was working in the Hutt Valley, who had his fiancée Beryl Mathieson with him and Beryl's father and mother, who could become her own New Zealand parents at least for the day. They were warm and welcoming, and she felt safe and secure.

The Mathieson family turned on a genuine Kiwi meal for their two young visitors — roast lamb, pumpkin, kumara, potatoes and gravy followed by a steamed pudding. It was a completely new concept of food for Suzy and she loved it. The Mathiesons were good hosts and Suzy took a particular shine to Isaac Mathieson, Beryl's father. Feeling relaxed and at ease sufficiently to show her feelings, she perched on his knee, gave him a kiss and a hug and told him how much she liked him.

Her brothers were horrified. 'You don't do that in New Zealand,' they scolded her. It was the first inkling she had that manners might not be quite the same in her adopted country. In the Netherlands it was customary to sit on someone's knee and nobody thought anything of it. Dutch women together would always hold hands or walk arm in arm. Not in New Zealand. 'Don't wave your hands around, Suzy,' was a mantra she would hear for years.

Things were now working to plan. From Wellington she, Joop and a small group of the eager young immigrants who had left the ship now boarded the ferry for Lyttelton. Next they were on the train and heading south again.

The scarred, wooden railway seats were hard, there were no cushions, and with no fat on her bottom, it was an uncomfortable ride for Suzy. It was also distressing. At each stop, it seemed, another migrant would gather up his or her belongings, say a tearful and often frightened goodbye and step off the train into the unknown. The tight group of friends that had spent 42 days at sea sharing hopes, dreams, and occasional misgivings was slowly fragmenting. Everyone was crying, waving and calling out best wishes as one by one they were deposited at railway stations throughout the South Island.

It was part of the New Zealand government's assimilation plan. The officials wanted their new arrivals to look like New Zealanders, speak like them as soon as possible and to be pepper-potted throughout the country. That way, there would be no unhealthy 'foreign cells' and there would be general acceptance of the Dutch as good citizens. For some, in their strange new home, there would also be painful homesickness and loneliness.

By the time the train reached Invercargill after an 18-hour journey there were only Suzy and Joop left from the original group on board ship. They had arrived at what Suzy believed must be 'the end of the earth'. Invercargill at first glance seemed bleak, bare and empty of people. But there were prospects. Willy had organised a bed for Suzy with his father and mother-in-law and a job interview for her at the Bamboo restaurant.

Suzy, as it turned out, enjoyed Invercargill. She saw it as a wealthy town. It was quiet, spacious and safe. She admired the bustling wide streets and the parks, even if they were alarmingly deserted. But she was bemused by the stares of the local people, for suddenly she was the tallest and slimmest woman in the street — and quite possibly the best dressed. At first she felt like a freak and had to fend off questions about where she had come from.

'Have you been in a concentration camp?' some asked. 'You're so skinny.'

Her clothes were worthy of attention too. So much so that much of the wardrobe she had worked for so hard and carefully selected in the Netherlands, including a long angora coat, a hand-printed Italian skirt and a dress, was stolen.

New Zealand women, she noted, seemed mostly to wear pink hats and cardigans, navy blue suits and gloves. The men were outfitted in a boring uniform of monogrammed blazers, white shirts and black or grey trousers, and they carried lunch-boxes to work.

Willy took her to the Bamboo. It was a large and successful 150-seat restaurant owned by John Kirkland and patronised by well-off farmers and well-paid workers from the boats at Bluff. It boasted bamboo on the walls, lush carpet and good quality Formica tables. It was a splendid, provincial, steak-and-chips-and-salad sort of restaurant.

The interview with John Kirkland went well, with Willy doing most of the talking as Suzy's schoolgirl and last-minute-coaching English was not yet up to negotiating. She got the job and started the next day. Instead of Suze, which was considered to be too 'foreign', John Kirkland and his staff called her Suzy.

She was put in charge of a huge Italian espresso machine with eight handles, shown how it worked and how to make coffee, hot chocolate, tea and Milo and left to it. Suzy had been out for coffee often enough in Europe to know how things were done, so she settled in happily behind the hissing machine and became the Bamboo's barista. At last she was in business again. Orders from the eight waitresses flew in; the coffees, hot chocolates, teas and cups of Milo flew out. She claimed her domain and shooed the others away. She might not know how to speak English properly, but she could make a European quality cup of coffee.

After a week she received her first pay. By this time, Suzy had rented a room for £6 a week. For her first week's work at the Bamboo, she had earned £8.15s. She looked at the pay slip in disbelief.

'Phut! I'm going back to Holland. I'm not going to stay here.'

She screwed up the envelope, threw the money on the floor and walked out. Did New Zealanders have no idea about waitressing at all?

Willy took her back to the Bamboo and acted once more as negotiator. John Kirkland, Willy and Suzy sat down to try to work out a solution. Insulted and shocked by what she understood of the conversation, Suzy was hysterical. She wasn't going to work for that kind of money. No way, she shouted. She was earning big money in the Netherlands.

Willy spoke to her in Dutch. 'Do you know how much I earn? I've got children to support and I get £13.10 for a six-day week.'

'Well, fool you,' snapped Suzy. 'I wouldn't!'

John Kirkland and Willy talked the situation over and over, while Suzy, silenced by the unfamiliar language, sat fuming. A conclusion was reached. Like it or lump it. She would work six days a week for 10 hours a day and get £14 clear, and she was not to breathe a word about her wages to anybody else. Deal done.

Suzy went back to work. When the restaurant wasn't so busy, she helped out at the tables, lent a hand in the kitchen and did some of the cleaning. She wasn't frightened of hard work; in fact, she enjoyed it — just as long as she was paid what she was worth. John Kirkland installed her behind the till when he wasn't there and trusted her sufficiently to have her do the banking. She was now the Bamboo's manageress.

Joop was living in a boarding house and working at the

freezing works. Suzy set about building her own 'home to come home to' in her rented room. It was furnished with the bare necessities — a bed, a small table, a chair and a wardrobe — to which she added a little Persian rug she had brought from home. She bought a lamp and a pot plant, hung prints on the walls and built a book case with bricks and planks of wood. Occasionally the other waitresses would visit her cosy little room, perching on the chair or the bed for a cup of coffee and an out-of-work chat.

She settled into a routine, bought a Raleigh bicycle and rode it to work, calling in on the way for a coffee at the Genevieve coffee bar with its picture of the Darracq motorcar, star of the 1953 British film. Suzy enjoyed the ambience of the little coffee bar and her new independence. She continued to rent her room for three months; then she and Joop joined a group of other Dutch young men and women who had arrived in Invercargill before them, and together hired a large house and set up a flat.

Right: Suzy arrived in New Zealand in 1960. She took a job as a waitress at the Bamboo restaurant in Invercargill.

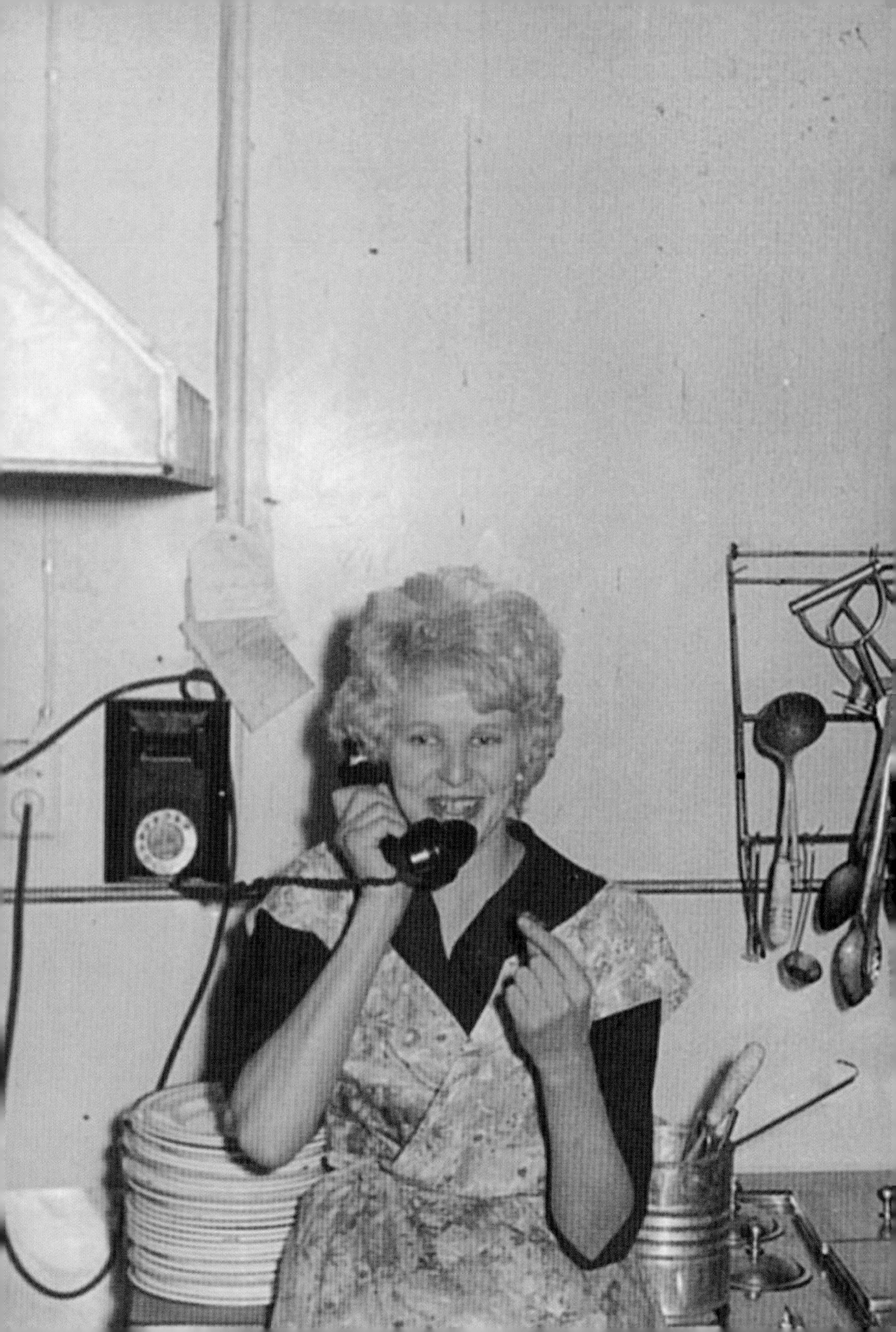

Above: At home in the Invercargill flat.

Right: Taking a break at the Bamboo.

Suzy was now settling into her new home with more confidence. With Willy and June nearby, pleasant flatmates and a secure job she was making a new life. Then, on 25 January 1961, Hendrikus, aged 64 years, suffered a heart attack and died in his sleep. A telegram arrived with the news for Suzy and Willy the day after his death. A few days later an aerogramme from Hendrikus arrived in Invercargill.

To his much loved and sorely missed young daughter on the other side of the world Hendrikus wrote:

Dear Daughter
Everything is still the same here. It is just that at the moment I am not able to do much. Herman does all the selling. Yesterday we went to Zwolle, there were very few vegetables but a lot of fruit. We had two crates of apples and pears and six of red cabbages and two of Savoy cabbages. Onions cost 22 cents gone up by 10 cents in one week. Yes it is already pretty cold. Last night it was eight below zero, but in the daytime it is pretty sunny, about zero degrees. One afternoon I was going to chop down that big pear tree because it died last year because of the drought. All of a sudden I had a pain around the region of the heart and I had to stop. When I ride fast on my bike I also get it. If things don't change soon I will have to visit the doctor and see what he says. But that is going to cost money.

We recorded a tape on a tape recorder on Sunday. Betsie took one with her from Almelo. We then all talked a little. I had invited Bart Aalders and his wife but they didn't show up. I went over there on Saturday night. He and his wife were alone in the shop and his wife could hardly stand. They no longer have anyone to help out, so that's pretty hard. Toos is having her birthday today and we're having a party tonight.

Toos is already 29, how time flies. Betsie has a healthy, big boy, he already weighs 21 pounds. He is hungry all day but he never cries. It's Marietje's turn in February, as well as the wife of Hennie. I never saw that coming. That sure is going to be something!

How are things with you? Everything all right? I would like to write to Joop as well, but I don't think that will happen today. Unlike us, you don't have so many things to worry about over there. Gerard also has wedding plans and now has all his stuff in the barn, because when they are married they need their own things. Toos has sent the tape recorder by boat, so that may take a while before it arrives. It also includes some photos for Willie. Give my regards to Joop from all of us and I hope you are happy. Toos is very busy, so doesn't have time to write.

Anyhow, best wishes and talk to you soon.

Suzy was deeply shocked by her father's death. She hadn't known that he was ill and his death was totally unexpected. Coming so soon after her departure from the Netherlands amidst his obvious distress, it was a heavy burden to bear, and she cried herself to sleep night after night. Invercargill's skies seemed impossibly grey.

Without her father constantly in the background with his advice and his encouragement, she now had to think seriously about her own future. Joop, she was convinced, would never be her husband, Willy and Jan had New Zealand families and responsibilities of their own and her other brothers and sisters had their own lives and futures in Europe. As there was nobody to look after her right now and because it was clear that she would have to look after herself for the rest of her life, she determined that she should get on with it.

While she liked Invercargill, it was still a small town and it seemed unlikely that it would develop much more in the near future. To make money, Suzy decided, you needed more people. She was going to have to move.

She had been in Invercargill nine months when she was required in Wellington. Beryl and Jan were about to be married, and Suzy was to be a bridesmaid. There were dresses to be fitted and duties to be carried out. It was a happy time. Beryl and Jan were obviously in love and everyone at the wedding was friendly and relaxed. It was good to be part of the Mathieson clan again and Wellington cast its spell on her once more. It was a real city. There were more people there, brighter lights, taller buildings and plenty of opportunity to make money. Suzy returned to Invercargill and handed in her notice.

John Kirkland was taken aback. He didn't want to lose his manageress.

'You can't leave, you're under a two-year contract with the government,' he told her.

'Oh well, I'll tell you what, I'm not. I am a free immigrant and you can't keep me here against my will,' Suzy snapped back.

Joop, who had already resigned from his own job at the freezing works, had gone to Wellington a month before, so, she reasoned, she could stay with him until she found her feet. She packed her bags and headed north.

It was another leap of faith. Suzy knew that to survive in this new country she was going to have to work hard. While she had only helped out a few times at Joop's father's restaurant, she had closely watched European waitresses in action in the city. She knew they were well trained, they routinely earned good money augmented by plenty of tips, and were valued highly by their employers. And she had the considerable weight of the Dutch coffee trade behind her.

For the trip north she bought a BMW Isetta, and squeezed her possessions and a passenger into the little car and drove out of Invercargill. Her 'co-pilot' was a Dutch friend who had a wife and children and was keen to explore the idea of transferring his young family to the capital city.

Joop, meanwhile, had set up house in Hill Street in Wellington with a group of four Dutch friends, and Suzy assumed that she could have a room there too. But the young men weren't that keen on having her stay for long. Her passenger, who stayed for a week, decided Wellington was far too busy for him and returned to Invercargill. Undaunted by the circumstances and convinced of new opportunities in Wellington, Suzy began searching for a job and a home of her own.

The immigration officials had been right and there was plenty of work for waitresses in New Zealand. She liked the look of the Parisienne restaurant in the Imperial Building at 43 Dixon Street and applied for the advertised job, adding that she could start straight away but wouldn't work for under £14 for a six-day week because that was what she was paid in Invercargill. The owner, Dimitri Voulgaris was doubtful. He had £12 in mind.

'All right, you try me for a week and see if you think I'm worth it,' Suzy told him.

After a week he hired her at £14 and she kept the tips.

Above: Suzy and her BMW Isetta head north from Invercargill in 1961.

The next step was to find somewhere suitable to live. 'Always have one good outfit to go out in and always have a good address to live in,' Hendrikus had once instructed her.

I want a nice home at a good address,' Suzy told her Wellington lawyer, who suggested she consider a large, fully-furnished house at 112 Oriental Parade that was available for lease at 12 guineas a week.

Suzy inspected the property, liked what she saw and took the lease. She persuaded Joop and his friends, who were all working on the wharves, to join her. They would all sign the lease, she informed the five young men, and they would each have a large room. Suzy would take the small room and do the housework and cooking, eat at work and live rent free.

So, there was a new and busy routine to be mastered. Each morning before she went to the Parisienne, she set the breakfast table for everyone; then when they had all gone to work she did the cleaning and washing and set the table again, and prepared the evening meal. Her duties completed, she showered, dressed and walked from Oriental Parade to Dixon Street — to save the nine pence bus fare — and started work before 11 a.m..

Right: When Suzy arrived in Wellington she took the lease on this large, fully-furnished house at 112 Oriental Parade which remained her home for the next three years.

At the restaurant, she set the tables for the lunchtime opening and waited on customers. At 4 p.m. Joop would pick her up in her car or she would hurry back by herself to Oriental Parade during her own meal break and put the dinner on for her 'boarders'. By 5 p.m. she was back at the restaurant to work the evening shift until the Parisienne closed at 9 p.m. and the cleaning was done. Once a week she treated herself to an *Australasian Post* magazine that she read over a coffee at the nearby Chez Lilly coffee bar and restaurant in Dixon Street before she started work. It was her routine for the next few years.

Suzy was fulfilling her father's wishes. She certainly had one good outfit to go out in and Oriental Parade was definitely a good address. She enjoyed the work at the Parisienne, but it was only the means to an end as she still had her heart set on running her own business, and for that she needed to earn more money.

Two additional opportunities presented themselves and she took them both. The first was a night-time cleaning job, arranged by a customer, with a group of Samoan women who picked her up from the Parisienne and took her with them to clean offices on the Terrace between 11 p.m. and one in the morning. She liked the camaraderie. The women were fun and the work was easy but she was unimpressed with the wages. When the Austrian owners of Chez Lilly, Kurt and Lily Blum, offered her part-time hours at nights after she had finished at the Parisienne, she took them instead.

The Parisienne proved to be an excellent training ground. Mr and Mrs Voulgaris were Bulgarian, the other waitress was Polish, and the restaurant had a distinctly European air about it. Flora Voulgaris cooked set meals that were predominantly Continental and included such classics as goulash, curries, and Wiener schnitzel — along with the ubiquitous steaks.

It was more than the food, however, that Suzy observed closely and that would influence her own business practices. Flora Voulgaris arrived at the restaurant each day dressed in a hat, high-heeled shoes and well-cut clothes. In the kitchen she put on overalls and worked hard throughout the day. At the end of work, she took off her overall, patted her hair carefully and left. She was always polite to her kitchen staff and courteous to the waitresses, and she made sure they always had clean tea towels to work with. She was, Suzy concluded, 'a real lady'.

Two doors away from the Parisienne, the very popular Chez Lilly, served good coffee and soups, freshly-baked bread, bratwurst, Wiener schnitzel, potato salads — and steaks. Customers bustled in and out during the day and in the evenings they queued down Dixon Street for a table.

In late 1962 Suzy made her next move. If people were prepared to line up for service at Chez Lilly, she figured, maybe the time was right and there was room for a new coffee bar in Wellington.

The seduction of France

Conversation in France was at its zenith. There were less eloquence and rhetoric than in '89. With the exception of Rousseau, there was no orator to cite. The intangible flow of wit was as spontaneous as possible. For this sparkling outburst there is no doubt that honor should be ascribed in part to the auspicious revolution of the times, to the great event which created new customs, and even modified human temperament — the advent of coffee.

Its effect was immeasurable, not being weakened and neutralized as it is today by the brutalizing influence of tobacco. They took snuff, but did not smoke. The cabarét was dethroned, the ignoble cabarét, where, during the reign of Louis XIV, the youth of the city rioted amid wine-casks in the company of light women. The night was less thronged with chariots. Fewer lords found a resting place in the gutter. The elegant shop, where conversation flowed, a salon rather than a shop, changed and ennobled its customs. The reign of coffee is that of temperance. Coffee, the beverage of sobriety, a powerful mental stimulant, which, unlike spirituous liquors, increases clearness and lucidity; coffee, which suppresses the vague, heavy fantasies of the imagination, which from the perception of reality brings forth the sparkle and sunlight of truth; coffee anti-erotic.

Histoire de France, Jules Michelet (1867)

The French were introduced to coffee as early as 1644, and the first commercial importation of coffee to France came in bales from Egypt in the early 1660s. The people of France 'wanted to know this Oriental beverage, so much vaunted, although its blackness at first sight was far from attractive', wrote Édelestan Jardin in *Le Caféier et le Café* (1895). In 1671 they set up their first coffee house, or café after the French word for coffee, in Marseilles, and others followed. So did the age-old controversy.

This time the threat came from the medical fraternity. The rapid growth in numbers of coffee houses, the physicians reasoned, was cause for alarm.

'Rubbish,' replied the coffee crowd.

Matters came to a head in 1769 when the physicians of Marseilles set a young student, who was about to be admitted to the College of Physicians, the task of disputing the good or ill of coffee. The thesis, though chilling in its claims that coffee induced palsies, impotence and leanness, fell largely on deaf ears. Coffee's popularity soared and the merchants of Marseilles and Lyons began to import green coffee by the shipload.

The people of Paris cottoned on. In 1672, a coffee booth set up by an Armenian called Pascal traded briskly from a tent at the springtime fair of St Germain, dispatching young Turkish waiters into the crowds to peddle the drink in small cups on trays. Pascal followed up this initial success with a small coffee shop near the Pont Neuf which languished for want of sit-down customers; but, heartened by his experience at the St Germain fair, he plied a successful trade in coffee-to-go hawked door-to-door through the Parisian streets and served from large coffee jugs heated by lamps.

Other coffee houses tried their luck in the city and met with equal disinterest from the smart set. Wines and beers were in favour at court, and the coffee houses, which most closely resembled the lower style of Oriental establishment, were left to survive on the custom of the poorer classes and foreigners.

Then everything changed. Canny French merchants, aware of coffee's successes elsewhere, set up spacious and elegant apartments serving refreshments, and the fashionable crowd was convinced. As in Italy before them, women were among the customers.

It was François Procope, a Parisian lemonade vendor with a royal licence to sell spices, ices, barley water and other refreshments, who adapted the Oriental coffee house to the café that the French would take to their hearts. He was a shrewd operator. He added coffee to his menu in 1689, and opened a new coffee house opposite the recently-opened Comédie Française to attract high class patronage. The strategy worked.

Café de Procope became the popular gathering place of the most prominent French actors, authors, dramatists and musicians of the 18th century. Aspiring writers, actors and musicians mixed with luminaries such as Voltaire, Rousseau, Beaumarchais and Diderot, and debated the issues of the day. In 1789, at the beginning of the French Revolution, Café de Procope was the scene of coffee, chess and heated political debate amongst its patrons including Marat, Robespierre, Danton, and the young Napoleon Bonaparte. When American Republican Benjamin Franklin died in 1790, Café de Procope went into deep mourning, swathed in black bunting inside and out.

Suzy wasn't the only one monitoring eating trends. New Zealand, it seemed, had been growing more sophisticated and others, too, had noticed the increased interest in good food and service and the popularity of the coffee house. Caliban writing in the *New Zealand Listener* had observed, with tongue in cheek, that in 1957 it was 'now possible, and it is becoming increasingly popular, to dispense with tea and cakes, stout and oysters'.

The New Zealand social historian of 50 years hence looks like having to reserve at least a page or two in his book to coffee. And, though no doubt a little premature, it's already possible to reflect a little on what has so far occurred: on the amazing proliferation in our cities of dimly-lit, 'atmospheric' coffee shops (or to be strictly up-to-date, coffee 'bars').

There was a time when such a thing would have been frowned upon universally. Tea (a staple diet) was consumed with as little thought for alternatives as water is used for washing. If you wanted to break the morning or afternoon in two, you made for the 'tearooms', where you would be presented with tea in a silver service flanked by three plates of food: sandwiches, scones and ornamental éclairs. This was quite a ritual limited to the daylight hours. After 4.00 p.m., these tearooms, for all practical purposes, ceased to exist. And if in the evening you wanted a rough substitute, a milk bar, a grillroom or at worst a pie cart would have to do ... these coffee bars have steadily begun to usurp the function of their more staid and less imaginative antecedents.

They have come with liberal quantities of posters displaying the provocations of Cannes and the Champs Elysees. They have come with venetian blinds, Chinese prints, Japanese fishnet, American music, Swedish wallboard, and French waiters. And they have come with a number of recipes for coffee and a welcome disregard for the time. In them you can lounge (in low cane chairs) or perch (on elevated iron and plush stools). No longer need lovers, deep in conversation, pace deserted streets. They may now talk in muted tones over steaming coffee.

The following year, the magazine picked up the theme of the 'exotic' again, adding that, 'True, Wellington has one main-street establishment called simply the Espresso Coffee-Bar, but such austerity is not the rule'.

Little more than two years ago, coffee shops ... were unknown in New Zealand. Today they are as much a part of the local scene as the T.A.B. — and almost as ubiquitous; the latest means of adding colour and glamour to our lives (and siphoning off our superfluous purchasing power). With their concealed or subdued lighting, pot-plants and foam-rubber or cane upholstery, they create on this otherwise rugged frontier an atmosphere of continental-style luxury happily independent of the overseas exchange situation.

They are the home of the atmospheric gimmick — the fishnet curtaining, the low-wattage electric bulb, the tropical fish-tank, the contemporary print — for atmosphere, too, is part of their stock-in-trade ...

In *Around New Zealand in Eighty Cups*, a slim volume 'based on eyewitness accounts, personal experiences, and fact', Rob MacGregor aka Robin Geoffrey added his own take on the new trend, describing 'the people, the decor, the music, the atmosphere, and sites of New Zealand coffee lounges'.

Throughout the length and breadth of New Zealand hundreds of vacant attics, cellars, rooms, offices, and what have you, have and are being subjected to the amateur and professional artists, painters and wallpaper specialists in a creative attempt to wave the magic wand of continental influence and give to the public surrounds where a simple cup of coffee can be sipped whilst a mural of some individual's artistic mind peers on.

Yes, like the daisies in the meadow, coffee lounges are springing up all over the Dominion, ranging from the elaborate and palatial lounge deluxe to the smoke filled speakeasy of a back street hideaway. The coffee lounge, or in other words a place where you and I can lounge over a cup of coffee with our feet resting on a South Pacific raffia mat, elbows daintily placed on a two, three, or four legged table. In some cases the tables have no legs at all, and one finds him or herself flat out on a linen covered cushion with feet pushed almost into a neighbour's saucer.

Suzy had worked hard and saved hard, and when a shop came up for lease at 292 Wakefield Street, she and Joop decided to take it and set up a coffee bar. She saw it as a chance at last to work for herself, to be her own boss. 'It is better to sell shoe polish door to door than to be a top secretary for a big company. You earn more and you have your freedom,' Hendrikus had told her.

The now vacant shop had previously repaired motor cycles and required a great deal of work before it was transformed into Suzy's idea of a coffee bar. However, if Suzy could get a loan, and if Joop could work part-time in the coffee bar, and if Suzy could keep on working at Chez Lilly at nights, they could afford to get started. Their original flatmates had moved out now and the arrangement of Suzy cooking and cleaning was finished. When new flatmates moved in Joop shared his large room and Suzy kept her small room and now paid her share of the rent like everybody else.

First they had to buy the lease to take over the shop. The previous owner had applied for an 'eating house' licence for 50 customers, but the application had lapsed before the restaurant was established. There was much to sort out. Suzy approached MARAC Finance for a loan to start her own business but was turned down.

'Look,' she said, 'I've saved almost £2,000 in the 18 months I've been in Wellington. Surely I can have £5,000.'

They were impressed with her savings and asked for a guarantee. She couldn't provide one, but she assured them they would have their money back as soon as she could earn it. That wasn't the point, they said, but gave her a five-year loan at 28 per cent interest anyway. She was as good as her word. She paid them back — whether they liked it or not — within the year.

The Windmill, she decided, would be a relaxed, cosy and very inviting coffee bar. The site on the corner of Wakefield Street and Cambridge Terrace was strategic, as the flower and produce markets were over the road and the businesses of Courtenay Place were not far away. Based on what she had learned already from working at the Bamboo, the Parisienne and Chez Lilly, Suzy designed the new coffee bar. It had to be practical, modern and relatively cheap.

The shop had only a small floor area, so a builder was contracted to construct a kitchen upstairs, a dumb waiter to transport the food downstairs, a new counter and new stairs. Furniture and a navy blue carpet had to be bought on time payment, and lamps with attractive lampshades — in the Continental style — had to be selected. A £50 second-hand record player was purchased to add to the ambience. Coffee and food suppliers were sourced and staff hired.

Suzy and Joop were both registered as the building permit owners, and Joop was registered as the builder. To save money and time they did the decorating themselves, applying brown hessian to one wall and blue to another.

Above: Joop Alders and Suzy opened the Windmill coffee bar on the corner of Wakefield Street and Cambridge Terrace on 22 July 1962. The interior (next page) is in Continental style.

Suzy worked nights at Chez Lilly until the last week before the opening so that she could paint the interior of the Windmill during the day. By the time everything was bought and in place, the money from MARAC had all gone and Suzy was surviving on a diet of potato crisps, fish and chips and Coca Cola. It was the first time she had been hungry in New Zealand and she was frightened. But, she told herself firmly, it would be worth it.

On 22 July 1962 the Windmill opened and from 6 a.m., when the workers and buyers from the markets came for coffees, until closing time around midnight, the little coffee bar was packed.

When he finished work for the day, Dimitri Voulgaris, to whom Suzy had never really warmed, walked down from the Parisienne in Dixon Street to the Windmill in Wakefield Street and placed £25 on the counter. It was, he said, to wish Suzy good luck on her first day. It was a completely unexpected gesture of goodwill from a man who, in a sense, was now her business rival; it was also a mark of recognition from one successful European businessperson to another. Exhausted and at an emotional tipping point, she thanked him and burst into tears.

Suzy worked downstairs serving customers and managing the till. A waitress carried trays of food, seated the customers and cleared the tables, a Dutch cook worked in the kitchen and Joop helped out where he could around his work commitments at the wharves. Lunchtimes were particularly frantic, with soup, toasted sandwiches, pizza, salads, bratwurst and frankfurters whizzing downstairs from the kitchen. All day a Dutch menu of potato salad, egg-ham-and-bread *uitsmijters* and rich cakes baked by Herman van de Bregge was served to a steady stream of customers and washed down with gallons of coffee.

Every day now, the Windmill was buzzing. An extra kitchen hand had to be hired and still more staff were required. Joop worked there for longer hours, but it was Suzy who was in charge.

One day when the coffee bar was full of customers and the orders were not arriving quickly enough for Suzy's liking she stormed up the stairs and said to Joop, who was working in the kitchen, 'For, God's sake hurry up. The people are waiting.'

Joop turned with butter in his hand and calmly pushed it in to Suzy's face where it dripped down on to her black dress. She returned down the stairs, wiped her face and dress and continued working.

'Sorry, accident happened,' she told her bemused customers.

Suzy hired university students to serve customers in the evenings until closing time and to prepare the food for the next day. Then there was the cleaning to be done until about one in the morning, and she was back at the markets for fresh food and flowers at five. One night, when she was closing up by herself, a man appeared behind her in the darkness and demanded that she hand over the money. Wakefield Street was empty. Terrified, she turned the key in the lock and ran for her life.

It was a crazy existence but Suzy was young and strong, and she has always had the ability to wake every morning refreshed and positive.

Whatever her cares from the day before, she reasoned, things would turn out better tomorrow. The flat at 112 Oriental Parade was only a place to shower, wash clothes and sleep — briefly. The Windmill was Suzy's new home and the business was her life.

But it was a relatively lonely life. For three years a fear that the move to New Zealand had been foolish had niggled away and her father's death had threatened her fragile confidence. Even if he hadn't been there in person he could be relied on for advice. Hendrikus had kept in touch through letter-writing, and she had assumed he would be there when she finally went back to the Netherlands. She felt completely cut off from both her family and her culture.

Hard work, she decided, was not just physical toil but an emotional workout as well. To survive she would have to harden herself and to some extent distance herself from other people. There was little time to make her own friends now anyway with the Windmill's long hours. Joop, who frequently left her at the coffee bar while he spent time with his mates, clearly was not ready to settle down and take on responsibilities. Besides, he was suggesting he might return to the Netherlands before long.

The people closest to her were the staff members who worked for her — a challenging position for a young woman who was often their junior in years but was also their boss. Added to her sense of being isolated was the responsibility she felt towards the people she employed.

People who had never had to work for survival — just to survive and to make sure they had enough money for themselves and others — could never understand, she concluded. If you're an accounts clerk or a shop assistant you work for someone, but if you have your own business it's quite different. You have responsibilities towards the people who are employed by you, and for the bills and the rent. Sometimes she wondered where the next dollar was coming from and it seemed that her back was against the wall.

At times she felt let down by the country that had encouraged her to come but had quite deliberately separated her from her friends. She knew many other immigrants felt the same. They were lonely. They were alone. The only possible solution to it all, she decided, was to push the sadness aside and to work, work, work.

Coffee versus beer

It is disgusting to notice the increase in the quantity of coffee used by my subjects, and the amount of money that goes out of the country in consequence. Everybody is using coffee. If possible this must be prevented. My people must drink beer. His Majesty was brought up on beer, and so were his ancestors, and his officers. Many battles have been fought and won by soldiers nourished on beer; and the King does not believe that coffee-drinking soldiers can be depended upon to endure hardship or to beat his enemies in case of the occurrence of another war.

Coffee and beer manifesto, Frederic the Great (1777)

The Germans were slow to adopt coffee despite their early knowledge of the drink through traveller Leonhard Rauwolf, who reported home in 1582 that coffee houses were numerous in the Orient. When introduced, coffee was an expensive commodity and was, at first, reserved for the elite, who tried to convince the grumbling lower classes that its consumption would lead to sterility. Besides, tradition ran deep, and beer had always been the German drink of choice.

Nevertheless, the first German coffee house was opened by an English merchant in Hamburg in 1679 and was rapidly followed by others throughout the country. During the second half of the 18th century, coffee was beginning to take the place of flour soup and warm beer at German breakfast tables. Alarmed by this turn of events, Frederick the Great issued his coffee and beer manifesto in a campaign against wholesale drinking of coffee.

The people were unimpressed. The king tried another tack, establishing a coffee monopoly designed to bring his subjects to heel. He established royal coffee roasters, issued special roasting licences to preferred members of the upper classes, sold coffee beans from the royal supplies and installed 'coffee-smeller' spies in the streets.

It was a familiar pattern. The public coffee houses were driven underground; the people resumed their coffee habit.

The Elector of Cologne, Maximilian Frederick, followed suit in 1784 issuing his own extraordinary manifesto:

To our great displeasure we have learned that in our Duchy or Westphalia the misuse of the coffee beverage has become so extended that to counteract the evil we command that four weeks after the publication of this decree no one shall sell coffee roasted or not roasted under a fine of one hundred dollars, or two years in prison, for each offense.

Every coffee-roasting and coffee-serving place shall be

closed, and dealers and hotel-keepers are to get rid of their coffee supplies in four weeks. It is only permitted to obtain from the outside coffee for one's own consumption in lots of fifty pounds. House fathers and mothers shall not allow their work people, especially their washing and ironing women, to prepare coffee, or to allow it in any manner under a penalty of one hundred dollars.

All officials and government employees, to avoid a penalty of one hundred gold florins, are called upon closely to follow and to keep a watchful eye over this decree. To the one who reports such persons as act contrary to this decree shall be granted one-half of the said money fine with absolute silence as to his name.

Many 'coffee-smellings' were reported and much unhappiness was the result. As expected both schemes were flops and the German coffee houses opened their doors once again.

Vienna — 1683

Paris — 1689

Boston — 1689

New York — 1696

Joop did go home. For some time he had been unhappy with what he had found in New Zealand, and while he had made good friends and had never been without a job, he believed the country had too few people and too many sheep.

He and Suzy agreed to sell the Windmill in October 1964 and split the profits. They had shared a great adventure that had taken them to the other side of the world, and they parted as friends. Joop returned to the Netherlands, and Suzy weighed up the situation. Apart from her two brothers, there was little tying her to New Zealand now, so she was free to return to Europe — not to the Netherlands yet but to a fresh start in Spain. She was relatively wealthy, with over £5,000 in her bank account. She began negotiations, through her Wellington lawyer, with a real estate agent to buy a hotel, with a house included, just outside Barcelona.

But then there was Tom.

Tom van der Kwast had become a regular customer at the Windmill and was a friend of Joop. They often played chess together. Tom had recently suffered a stroke and was left partially paralysed with Bell's palsy and forced to sip his coffee at the Windmill through a straw. He was good natured and charming, and Suzy had grown to enjoy his company. He was separated from his wife and negotiating a divorce, and if she waited a while longer, he told Suzy, he would come with her to Spain.

Suzy was unsure. Things were moving fast. She had worked for three years for up to 18 hours a day with no holidays, and it was time for a break and some serious thinking. She drove to Taupo, then on to Rotorua for a rest.

Of course it was not only the food that had attracted Tom to the Windmill on a regular basis, but also Suzy's personality and what he describes as 'her innate beauty and goodness'. She was also tall, blonde and slim, and made anything she wore — however extreme — look a million dollars.

Above: In 1964, Suzy and Joop sold the Windmill and Joop returned to the Netherlands. Here, Suzy holidays in Rotorua while she plans her future.

Tom was nearly 10 years older than Suzy and had been in New Zealand since 1952. Like her he had suffered a childhood marred by the events of the Second World War, and because he had grown up in densely populated Amsterdam, the situation had been much worse.

His mother Petronella van Tol was a farmer's daughter and married Jan Jacobus van der Kwast, a farmer's son who had inherited the family business of farm and smallgoods manufacturing. Tom's father disliked both activities, preferring to spend his time playing his violin. With the war gnawing at Amsterdam there was no work and no food, and little time for music.

Tom had been at high school in 1944 when his education was abruptly interrupted. He had already been severely shaken when seven of his Jewish classmates had disappeared without warning. Now, the war was closing in. With no resources to heat the schools and with no teachers, no food or public transport, the schools were closed.

The family was starving, and young Tom was sent out on hunger trips, along with thousands of others, to scrape together some nourishment for his family. Families ate their pets. Children rubbed their fingers along the insides of rubbish bins in the hope of finding something edible. Amsterdam was bitterly cold. There was no coal, no wood, no running water or soap, and the sewers had long since given up. There were blackouts and curfews, overcrowding and starvation. So many people died in Amsterdam that, with a lack of coffins and transportation, it was impossible to bury them promptly. Somehow the van der Kwast family survived.

By April 1945 spring and warmer weather arrived. The schools reopened part way through the year, and Tom returned to his studies. There was enormous pressure on the education system now. Not only did the schools have to push the students through to make up the time they had lost during the war, but there were also increased numbers of students to teach, with the return of thousands of troops and Dutch nationals recalled from Indonesia. Tom finished his three years of high school amid the chaos and left aged 18.

His father's brother, who had immigrated to the United States and set up a flower nursery, had sent a letter through the Red Cross in 1945 inviting either of his van der Kwast nephews to join him. Here was Tom's chance. With a three-month permit he left Rotterdam on the Mormon-chartered ship *Leerdam* for New York City, then on to Connecticut as a horticultural 'student'. He applied for permit extensions and stayed for a year.

While he was convinced he was in the right part of the world, legitimising his position grew increasingly unlikely. It was not just the Dutch that were leaving their homes. Tens of thousands of European immigrants were pouring in to the United States through the official channels. Any independent application from Tom van der Kwast was thwarted by the sheer weight of numbers. Tom moved to

Springfield, Massachusetts and worked a series of odd jobs until the authorities caught up with him and he was given notice to leave the country within two weeks.

Back in Rotterdam he faced imprisonment for not completing his army service, having passed his physical examination before he had left for the United States. Aware that the Netherlands, under intense pressure or overcrowding, was actively encouraging its young people to leave and find a better life elsewhere, he arranged his own sponsorship by three farmers in New Brunswick, Canada, completed the necessary papers that exempted him from military service and he was on his way again.

After a year on an isolated, primitive, self-sufficient farm without electricity, a stint in a shoe factory in Frederickton, then 18 months working in Montreal, including six months at another flower nursery, and finally a year-long contract in Labrador on the Arctic Circle, Tom had enough money to head to New Zealand in pursuit of a high school sweetheart who was now living in Wellington.

Tom van der Kwast arrived in Evans Bay, after an eight-hour flight from Sydney on a TEAL Solent, on 22 December 1952. It was an auspicious arrival. The first commercial flying boat service between Sydney and Wellington had begun in 1950, its planes docking beside a small passenger terminal near Hataitai Beach. In 1954 the service ceased when conventional aircraft took over the Tasman Sea service. More than 50 years later Tom and other Solent enthusiasts would begin moves to install a memorial to the aircraft in Cog Park, close to where he stepped onto New Zealand soil for the first time.

When Tom arrived, in the week before Christmas, there was an advertisement in the newspaper for a gardener at the Wellington Botanic Gardens. He applied, was employed over the telephone and asked to report on 10 January. He started working with the begonias and a week later he was in charge of a nursery and 60,000 gladioli bulbs destined to be in peak flower for the tour of Queen Elizabeth II and the Duke of Edinburgh in January the next year.

Tom had received good training in his uncle's glasshouses in Connecticut. He knew how to grow poinsettias for the Northern Hemisphere's Christmas, geraniums for Memorial Day, lilies for Easter and chrysanthemums and carnations by the bucketful. He understood the importance of plant feeding, soil tests and temperatures, and could force plants or hold them back. He was a young man full of bravado and blessed with a practical streak and loads of common sense, and he applied them all to the task in hand. Obediently, the Queen's elegant gladioli flowered on time.

He left the job after three years to start up a landscape business at a time when Wellington was short of gardeners. The successful construction of a fountain led to commissions for garages and then houses, and by the time he met Suzy he had transformed himself into a builder.

Coffee house romance

Vienna cafés are famous, but the World War dimmed their glory. It used to be said that their equal could not be found for general excellence and moderate prices. From half-past eight to ten in the morning, large numbers of people were wont to breakfast in them on a cup of coffee or tea, with a roll and butter. Mélangé is with milk; 'brown' coffee is darker and a schwarzer is without milk. In all the cafés the visitor may obtain coffee, tea, liqueurs, ices, bottled beer, ham, eggs etc. ... For Vienna coffee, the liquor is usually made in a pumping percolator or by the drip process. In normal times it is served two parts coffee to one of hot milk topped with whipped cream. During 1914–18 and the subsequent post-war period, however, the sparkling crown of delicious whipped cream gave way to condensed milk, and saccharine took the place of sugar.

All About Coffee, William Ukers (1935)

The legend that surrounds the establishment of the first coffee house in Vienna is soaked in romance. It revolves around Franz George Kolschitzky, a Pole who had been an interpreter in the Turkish army and was in Vienna when, in 1683, Turkish troops attempted to capture the city. Vienna was surrounded by 25,000 Turkish tents housing 300,000 of Mohammed IV's men under the command of vizier Kara Mustapha, successor to Kolpili (he of the body bags in the Bosphorus). Kara Mustapha settled in for a long siege, sending out raiding parties and tunnelling under Vienna's walls.

In desperation, the Viennese sent out a scout to muster support from King John III Sobieski of Poland and Duke Charles of Lorraine, who arrived just in time, routed the Turkish army and saved Vienna. The popular story variously ascribes to Kolschitzky honours of serving the city as the heroic scout and as a surveillance agent who, familiar with Turkish customs and language, infiltrated the invading army and returned with knowledge invaluable for defence.

The Turkish invaders, who had packed for a long stay, fled leaving behind their 25,000 tents, 10,000 oxen, 5,000 camels, 100,000 bushels of grain, a good quantity of gold and sacks of strange beans. The booty was duly distributed and Kolschitzky, who was familiar with the charms of coffee from his days with the Turkish army, offered to take the unwanted sacks as his reward. After peddling cups of coffee in the streets, he reputedly opened the first public Turkish coffee booth in Vienna and is honoured in that city as the patron saint of coffee houses. The *kipfel*, or crescent-shaped roll traditionally served in Vienna with coffee, was first baked in 1683 during the Turkish siege and in the spirit of defiance. With a *kipfel* in one hand and a sword in the other, it was said, the Viennese would challenge Mohammed IV's troops. With coffee in their bellies they could take on the world.

For Suzy in Rotorua there were some major decisions to be made. As Joop had returned to the Netherlands there was now no boyfriend. She had no business in Wellington, no timetable to follow and no responsibilities for her staff. She could go to Spain. Or she could stay in Wellington.

Tom rang her at her hotel. Could he come up for the weekend to see her? When he arrived Suzy was having a casual drink with a group of men also staying in the hotel. She was relaxed and happy and enjoying the entertainment and male companionship. Tom's reaction surprised her. She had thought they were just friends but Tom, it seemed, had more serious intentions. 'When are you coming back to Wellington?' he asked.

So Suzy returned. She worked as a waitress for a fortnight helping out a colleague in the Caledonian Hotel near the Basin Reserve and then for a few months at the Capri coffee bar in Manners Street. By this time, a shop called Hansel and Gretel selling baby wear had become vacant in the McGill's Building in Willis Street, and Tom suggested that it would make a good coffee bar. Why not pool financial resources and go into business together? They could run the coffee bar together for maybe three years and then return to Europe. It was agreed.

The first six months of their friendship remained purely platonic, as Suzy was still wary of sexual relationships and was terrified of becoming pregnant. A year later when Tom moved into the house at 112 Oriental Parade with her she brushed aside any suggestions of marriage.

'Don't worry about marrying. I'm quite happy. I don't want to get married.'

The spectre of violence and poverty, large families and downtrodden people of her childhood was still very much alive. She would have none of it. Besides, she was too busy. There was a coffee bar to set up.

Suzy had firm ideas about what she wanted her new coffee bar to be like. There was to be nothing 'higglety-pigglety' about this one. It would be different. It would be hers. The food would be much better than that served in the other Wellington coffee bars and the hygiene would be of a better standard too.

There was crockery to be bought. Pots and pans, stoves and a bain-marie and all the accoutrements of a well fitted out commercial kitchen had to be sourced, selected and paid for. And if that wasn't enough, there was going to be a refrigerated salad bar — the first in Wellington.

Suzy wanted an ultra modern design with a cosy atmosphere and European flair that would attract a good clientele.

'You mix with the down and outers, you become a down and outer. You mix with the good people and you cannot help but become like them,' Hendrikus had told her.

Austrian architect Friedrich (Fritz) Eisenhofer and his New Zealand wife Helen often dined at Chez Lilly, which he had designed, and Suzy liked his work. One day, she met him in Cuba Street as he was walking to his office with his daughter and they stopped to chat.

'By the way, Fritz, my boyfriend and I are going to start a coffee bar and we wondered if we could make an appointment with you to discuss a design.'

Fritz Eisenhofer had studied architecture in Vienna and had been working on prefabricated house designs in Australia for a year before his contract finished. He had then decided to try his luck in New Zealand and arrived in Wellington in 1953 in the wake of the first group of Austrian tradesmen recruited to construct houses in Titahi Bay. In an effort to overcome a severe, post-war shortage of houses and qualified people to build them, the New Zealand government had entered into an agreement with Austrian company Thermobau Fertighäuser to supply 1,000 imported, pre-fabricated houses — 500 of them for Titahi Bay. Fritz Eisenhofer was employed by Unibuild Construction Limited — the company incorporated in New Zealand to oversee the project — and was put to work setting out the kitset houses.

Like most of the 194 Austrian tradesmen who came to New Zealand for the project and were subsequently offered permanent residency, he decided to stay. When Suzy met him he had completed a stint with the housing division of the Ministry of Works and had gone on to establish an architectural partnership in an office in Cuba Street with fellow Austrian Erwin Winkler.

Setting up a coffee bar in the narrow confines of the former baby wear shop was going to be a challenge, and as the weekly rent was £50 Suzy calculated that there would need to be seating for 50 to 60 customers. As there wasn't enough floor space downstairs there would have to be a new mezzanine, and there was a budget of only £12,000 for renovations and architect's fees. Fritz Eisenhofer settled at his drawing board to make the plan work.

Tom, in the meantime, had visited Wattie Davie and Son Ltd, one of Wellington's oldest real estate agencies, to secure the empty shop at 108 Willis Street and organise payment of the £3,000 key money.

'What are you going to do now?' Wattie Davie asked.

'Well, I don't know. I'm a builder. But I'm going to have to help out with the coffee bar, so I'll have to let the building go a bit.'

'Why don't you go into real estate?'

'I'll think about it,' was Tom's reply.

Two days later when he climbed the stairs again to the office above the boot-maker's shop on the corner of Courtenay Place and Allen Street in order to finalise the lease, there was the name 'van der Kwast' fixed to the door. So, the decision was made for him; when the coffee bar was built Tom would work in Willis Street for part of each day and in real estate for the rest.

Suzy had now taken a job at the Wardell's coffee lounge above the supermarket in Willis Street until her own coffee bar was finished. Wardell Bros & Co., Grocers and Provisions Merchant, was an old, established South Island firm that had set up a new branch in Wellington. Its coffee lounge was spacious, employed six staff members and was reputed to have the biggest turnover of any similar business in New Zealand at the time. Mrs Audrey Green was the manageress.

Suzy arrived at work at seven in the morning to organise the staff duties for the day. Mrs Green arrived at about 11 a.m. and took over the reins as manageress, working behind the till. It was then Suzy's job to serve customers, clear the tables and help out where needed.

She liked Mrs Green and the feeling was mutual. Audrey Green had Scottish roots, knew a great deal about food and retailing, and had an impressive library of overseas cookery books. Best of all, she was good fun.

The association with Wardell's gave Suzy an insight into the most efficient food suppliers in Wellington and the best purveyors of smallgoods in the country. She noted the names like Aalt Verkerk, who had established Verkerks, a European-style butchery and delicatessen business in Christchurch in 1956, and the Broeke family who introduced Continental meats to New Zealand around the same time under the brand name name 'Brooks'.

Audrey Green, who was fond of a drink, instructed Suzy

that alcohol didn't necessarily result in the misery and violence she had observed in Twente, taught her about food and kept her entertained with her wry repartee. As plans for the new coffee bar began to take shape, she decided it was time she had a change too. 'I wouldn't mind working for you,' she told Suzy. She was hired on the spot.

One neighbourhood at a time

The Green Dragon, the last of the inns that were popular at the close of the seventeenth century, was the most celebrated of Boston's coffee-house taverns. It stood on Union Street, in the heart of the town's business center, for 135 years, from 1697 to 1832, and figured in practically all the important local and national events during its long career. Red-coated British soldiers, colonial governors, bewigged crown officers, earls and dukes, citizens of high estate, plotting revolutionists of lesser degree, conspirators in the Boston Tea Party, patriots and generals of the Revolution — all these were wont to gather at the Green Dragon to discuss their various interests over their cups of coffee, and stronger drinks.

All About Coffee, William Ukers (1935)

Coffee houses modelled on their English and European counterparts were established in all the colonies and served coffee, chocolate and tea — and, often as not, alcohol as well, making them barely distinguishable from taverns. The first American coffee house is believed to be the London Coffee House, which opened for business in Boston in 1689, dealing in both coffee and books. In New York, where the Dutch founders initially preferred tea to coffee, the two-storey, wooden and yellow brick Kings Arms, the first coffee house in the city, was apparently shipped out from Holland.

These early institutions quickly became centres of business and political life, and shared social duties with the taverns, and, like the coffee houses of England and France, they were well known as 'seminaries of sedition'.

It was here that the colonists grumbled about England, and it was the association of England and tea that prompted America's longstanding loyalty to coffee. American Whigs argued in 1765 that, as colonists did not elect the members of the English parliament, they could not be taxed by them. The Stamp Act imposed by King George as a money-making device was repealed but not the right to tax, and instead, in 1767 duties were fixed on paints, oils, lead, glass and tea. The colonists resisted, refusing to import goods made in England and preferring to smuggle tea from Holland.

Faced with growing piles of tea in the English warehouses, the British East India Company appealed for permission to export tea and eyed up the American market. It was in the Green Dragon Coffee House in Boston that rebellious Samuel Adams and his co-conspirators hatched the plan for the Boston Tea Party of 1773 that would be the colonists' answer. The rebels boarded the ships in Boston harbour and hurled the tea cargoes into the waters of the bay.

It was a seminal moment. From then on coffee became

the preferred and indispensable caffeinated drink of the United States.

In the 1950s, American coffee houses underwent a spirited renewal. The evolution came courtesy of the Beat Generation who, adopting the traditions of the the *kahwe khaneh* of Mecca, brought entertainment back to the coffee house. The Beat Generation movement began in San Francisco's North Beach, Los Angeles' Venice West and New York's Greenwich Village, and the coffee houses became the centres for debate and performance. Lawrence Ferlinghetti and Allen Ginsberg read their poems in the coffee houses of San Francisco, and Bob Dylan shaped the music and attitudes of a generation in the coffee houses of Greenwich Village.

Almost 200 years after the rebels had tipped out the tea leaves, America had become saturated with coffee, and Starbucks — the 'third place' between work and home— had become its flagship. In the same spirit of colonisation shown by its coffee forebears of the 17th century, the Starbucks coffee houses have set out 'to inspire and nurture the human spirit — one person, one cup and one neighbourhood at a time'.

Wellington — 1939

In many ways Fritz Eisenhofer was perfectly suited for the task of designing Suzy's Coffee Lounge. Most of his clients were also Europeans — this was not necessarily his choice but more the result of a lingering Kiwi suspicion of 'aliens' and their strange ways. New Zealand-born Helen Eisenhofer was particularly sensitive to the undercurrent. 'Why did you marry a foreigner?' she was often asked.

Fritz Eisenhofer's architectural designs were different. In the 1958 Wainuiomata Parade of Homes organised by the Department of Housing, houses constructed by different builders for less than £3,000 were put on show for public inspection and criticism. The design of Winkler and Eisenhofer constructed by Unibuild was clearly out on its own, remarkable for the Winkler-Eisenhofer trademark clean lines and cost-efficient plan. The Kiwis who did acquire Eisenhofer-designed homes, however, tended to buy them directly from the builders, who had constructed them unsupervised from the architect's drawings and specifications, and often made modifications to suit the more conservative New Zealand tastes.

Unsurprisingly Winkler and Eisenhofer had already worked on a number of restaurants and coffee bars in Wellington for operators who were mostly Europeans themselves. The first was a shop conversion to the Austrian-owned restaurant and café Chez Lilly, where Suzy had previously worked and where, in the Continental style, Europeans gathered to drink coffee, share conversation and read overseas newspapers. Later, the pair of architects refurbished the Cuba Street building that featured a glass passage-way and, downstairs, housed book and florist shops and the new Swiss-owned Matterhorn restaurant, which they also designed. Upstairs were a bridal salon and the Winkler-Eisenhofer office. The eye-catching and novel forms of the classy Anne Barri shoe shop in Willis Street, with its inviting curved staircase and elegant hand-rail, and the Zodiac, the city's first licensed restaurant, with a black ceiling and suitably positioned 'star' lighting followed.

European immigrants who had arrived in the 1950s and 1960s to set up their new homes had been shocked by how little choice was available to them in the shops and how old-fashioned were the fittings and furniture on offer. For Erwin Winkler and Fritz Eisenhofer the answer was to create it all themselves. Every chair, table, counter, light fitting and floor covering for their commercial commissions had to be designed and custom made. Where wall surfaces were to be featured, it was often best to do the job themselves and the elegant sgraffito and sinuous screen figures at Chez Lilly were designed and built by Winkler and Eisenhofer.

Next page: (clockwise) The Anne Barri shoe shop and associated coffee bar was located a few doors away from Suzy's Coffee Lounge in Willis Street and was another innovative Winkler-Eisenhofer design. The popular Chez Lilly Dixon Street restaurant featured a sgraffito wall and a light and airy interior. Courtesy of Fritz Eisenhofer. (Photographer: Greig Royle Studio.)

Coffee

RESTAURAN
TEA

Like the *kahwe khaneh* of Mecca before them, these innovative Wellington establishments came hard up against bureaucratic muscle. There was trouble with the carpet and wall coverings at Chez Lilly because the City Council health and safety standards for eating establishments required hard floor coverings that could be washed down. Council officers at the time frowned too on any fashionable use of wall fabrics, particularly in cafés with the customary candle-in-the-bottle lighting.

The Matterhorn's outdoor dining area, designed for the owners Mr and Mrs Tresch and reputedly the first of its type for the city, caused a furore because, the council argued, bird droppings could contaminate the customers' food. The free form ferro-cement showroom window of the Anne Barri shoe shop and associated coffee bar slid right off the regulations books. Everything new was challenged, rejected and vigorously argued over.

Winkler and Eisenhofer's designs, however, were not created with a difference merely for the sake of causing a stir among council desks. On the contrary, they were created with the client in mind and were crafted to make a statement about the business they represented and to be eye-catching and memorable in what was, at the time, a generally dismal city environment. In short, they were designed to establish the sixties' equivalent of a 'brand'. The sculpted Chez Lilly entryway screen was inarguably a gesture of European sophistication. The small intimate dining area of the Matterhorn with its wooden chairs and tables, it's stone fireplace with a specially made and prematurely aged suspended copper pan and the dominating Matterhorn mountain photograph by Hubert Sieben was undoubtedly Swiss. Suzy's coffee bar in the McGill's Building, bracketed by a pharmacy and a butcher's shop, was going to be different again. It would be warm and inviting, it would have a European spirit. It should be cosy, she instructed, it should be '*gezellig*'.

'What should we call it, Suzy?' Fritz Eisenhofer asked, poised to add the name to the plans.

Suzy considered the question.

'Well everyone knows you as a waitress. Why not call it 'Suzy's'?'

So, Suzy's it was.

The small floor area and the high stud of the gutted shop space had already determined that the coffee bar would require a mezzanine and stairs. The convention of positioning the till at the front of the long, narrow space wasn't going to be possible here as the service counter needed also to be near the kitchen at the back. The solution was to install some tables on the left-hand side of the Willis Street entrance. On the right one table would accommodate customers, a long, angled food display could combine the innovative refrigerated salad bar groaning with the wide selection of food Suzy and Mrs Green were planning and a counter could be installed opposite the stair.

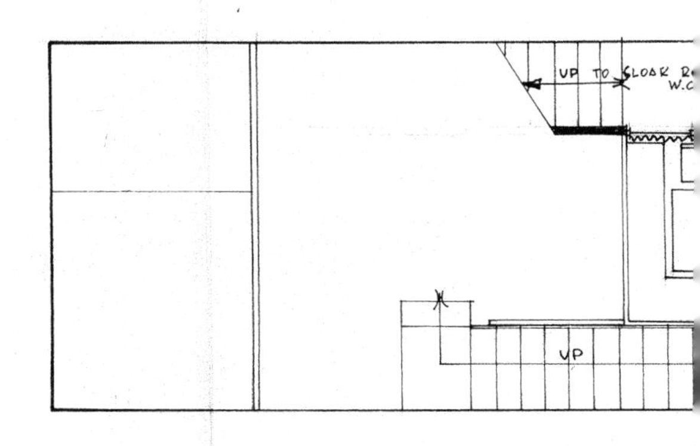

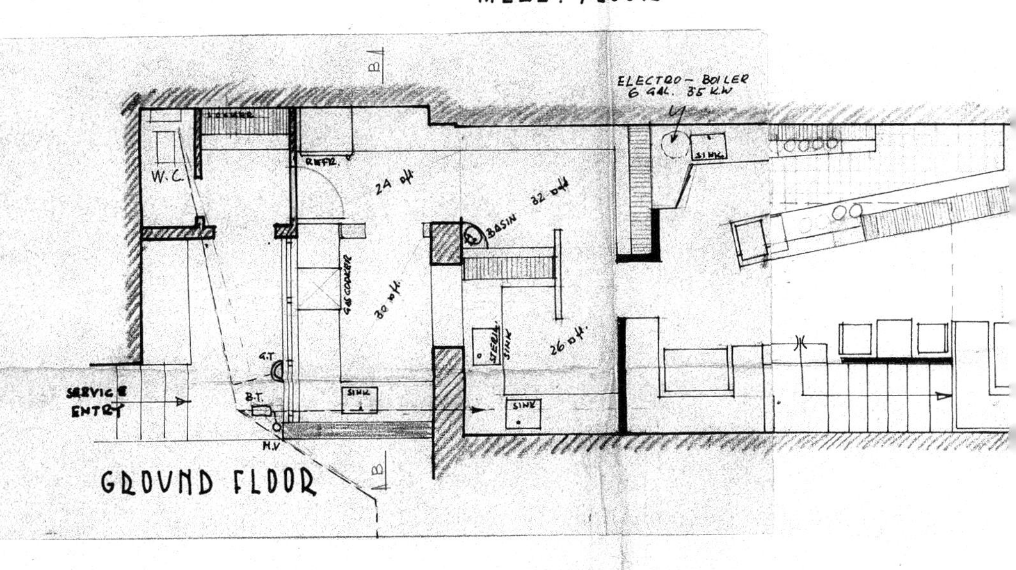

Above: Austrian architect Fritz Eisenhofer's shop alteration plans for Suzy's Coffee Lounge include a steel-framed window with wooden stars that challenged Council regulations. Courtesy of Fritz Eisenhofer. (00058-345-C14813, Wellington City Archives.)

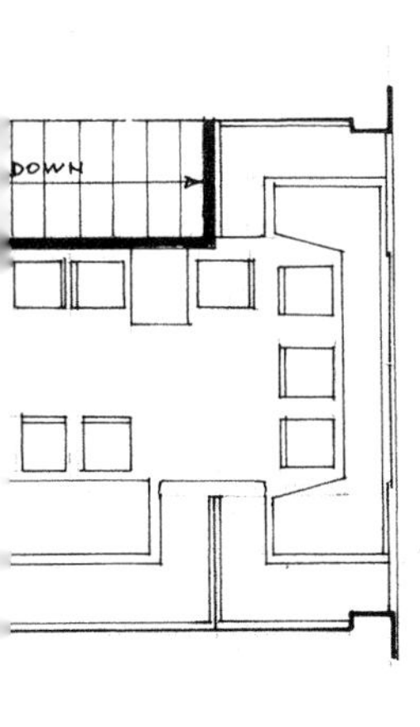

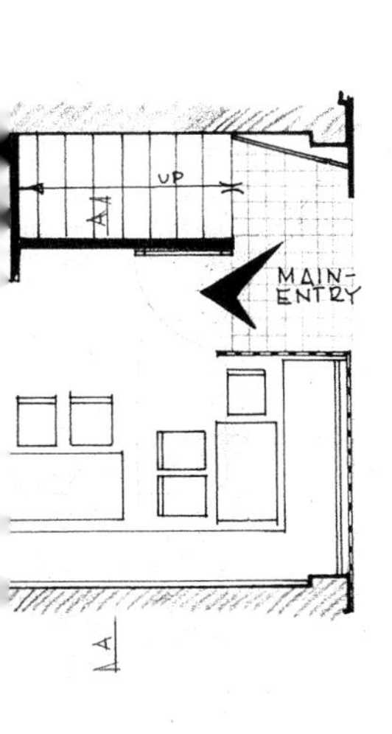

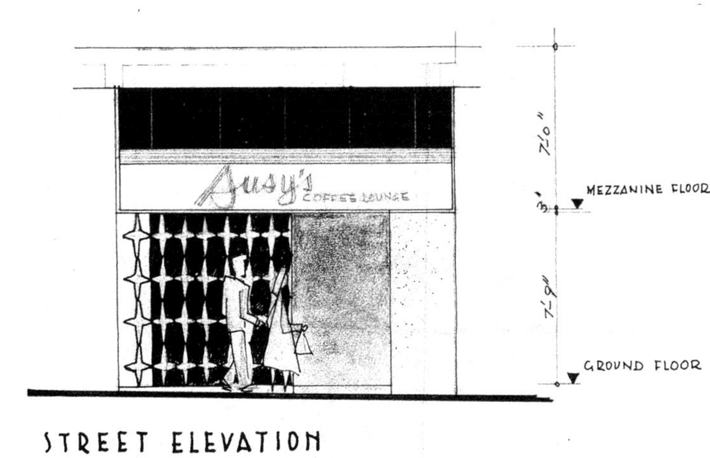

STREET ELEVATION

LIS STREET. SCALE : 1/4 INCH — 1 FOOT 321/B

ERWIN T. WINKLER
FRIEDRICH EISENHOFER ARCHITEC
106 CUBA ST. - WELLINGTON - P.O. Box 6239 - Tel. 55116.

A vibrant, striped carpet was designed by Fritz Eisenhofer and custom made by Felt and Textiles of NZ Ltd, an Australian company that had begun its New Zealand life making slippers in a factory round in Courtenay Place in 1929, and grew up to become Feltex Carpets.

A huge, copper art work was hung on the wall above the servery and a slick, Mondrian-style window in blue, green and yellow glass was installed over the entry to the kitchen. The bench-style seats and the tables were designed by Fritz Eisenhofer. The overall effect was to be clean and uncluttered with modern lines, and the 'horizontals, verticals and triangulars', so admired later by artist Rita Angus, were allowed to shine.

On the second floor was Suzy and Tom's spacious flat, with high ceilings and an open fire.

So far, everything was going to plan. Then, true to form, the coffee bar's street frontage caught the authority's punitive eye.

The Eisenhofer-designed, steel-framed window with its sleek, wooden stars was designed to screen customers from the street, achieving intimacy for the coffee bar and signalling the stylishness of the interior. In order to make the most of the available space, the window was slightly cantilevered over the footpath.

Tom, the pragmatic builder had got to work with the building team, G. Rabel & Co., and Fritz Eisenhofer the perfectionist architect had strolled round from 106 Cuba Street regularly to supervise the construction. Anything that wasn't quite straight or didn't meet the architect's specifications would have to be redone. Some sparks flew. The wooden stars in the front window had posed problems, but finally, each of them had been meticulously crafted by boat-builder Theo Hoedemaeckers, approved and installed and the whole steel frame had been set in concrete right on the street boundary.

The building inspectors, however, were not happy with the encroachment of the window on the footpath and told Tom to take the frame out and replace it. Tom, who is quite undaunted by authority, told them what he thought of their request. The building inspectors threatened court action. Tom rigged a light beam from the corner of Boulcott Street to the *Evening Post* building and proved — at least to himself — that the camera shop and the neighbouring butcher shop and probably two other shop fronts had windows that cantilevered over their boundaries too.

In July 1964 lawyers Scott, Hardie Boys and Morrison took up the van der Kwast cause, informing the chief building supervisor Mr Maynard that they would arrange to have the building line surveyed. Dismantling the window, they pointed out, would be 'disastrous for their clients, though they, of course, appreciated that this may be required'.

Disastrous indeed. The carpet was laid, the furniture was ready and Suzy was all but pouring the coffee from the new, shiny pots.

I. D. Maclean carried out the survey in August and Scott, Hardie Boys and Morrison enclosed his plan in their next letter to the chief building supervisor:

You will see that there is in fact an encroachment varying between 1 inch and 1 1/4 inches by the timber design on the outside of the window. Mr Maclean pointed out to us that the clearance of 5/8 inch between the building and the boundary line is measured at the base of the building and that the walls are mostly further back from the boundary than that.

On behalf of Suzy's Coffee Lounge Limited we ask that the Council allow this small encroachment. We think that you will agree that the shop window is most attractive in appearance and the encroachment is very small and we submit is not in any way a nuisance or obstruction to the pavement. The actual encroachment is less than had been originally thought and we think that this is probably because the walls of the buildings are further back from the boundary line than had been thought. Our clients have already been put to a good deal of expense and worry by this matter and we would most earnestly ask you to allow this small encroachment.

In September, the senior divisional engineer replied that, after all, he too thought 'the minor encroachment' was reasonable.

In the shadows of Willis Street, the spirits of rebel coffee house champions of earlier times — Shams and Hakam,

Floriano Francesconi, François Procope and Pasqua Rosée — chuckled and cheered.

Tom van der Kwast was issued with a £4.10 encroachment fee that he never paid.

Above: Audrey Green (front) and Suzy assemble behind the counter with one of the many teams of waitresses who worked at Suzy's Coffee lounge during its 23 years.

Right: On opening night Suzy and business partners Terry Rabel and Tom van der Kwast try out the brand new counter and the downstairs corner table.

Next page: Suzy sits at the table from which Rita Angus painted the view towards Willis Street. (photographer: Duncan Winder)

CONA
COFFEE

The French Maid

In Australia and New Zealand, English methods for roasting, grinding, and making coffee are standard. The beverage usually contains thirty to forty per cent chicory. In the bush, the water is boiled in a billy can. Then the powdered coffee is added; and when the liquid comes again to a boil, the coffee is done. In the cities, practically the same method is followed. The general rule in the antipodes seems to be to 'let it come to a boil,' and then to remove it from the fire.

All About Coffee, William Ukers (1935)

Chicory was first used with coffee in the Netherlands in 1770. Much of the coffee and chicory in New Zealand referred to by William Ukers was bought under the trade name of 'W. Gregg & Co', an enterprise that grew from the gold fields of Otago. William Gregg had emigrated from Northern Ireland to Australia in the 1850s to seek his fortune at the Ballarat gold fields. Lured by a substantial strike in Otago, he arrived in Dunedin in 1861, where he established a business as a coffee roaster, spice merchant and food manufacturer. By the time Ukers was explaining Kiwi coffee to the world, 'Gregg's' had grown to become a limited liability company, and in 1960, in an era of instant Maggi soups and instant Betty Crocker cake mixes, had introduced the first instant coffee to New Zealand taste buds.

Shortly after William Ukers had made his pronouncement on the state of the nation's coffee, however, there was one enterpreneur who was pioneering real coffee in a real coffee house in the capital city.

'Wellingtonians take their cup of coffee in a coffee bar so much for granted now that even those with long memories tend to forget that one man taught us the habit less than 30 years ago,' Fred Jones wrote in *The Dominion* in October 1967 under the headline 'He Taught Us How Coffee Should Taste'. The man was Dick Singleton. His coffee house was the French Maid at 356 Lambton Quay, next to Stewart Dawson's, and was first established at Rongotai in 1939.

Dick Singleton worked in a Wellington laboratory after leaving school, and then became a builder labouring for his father, then a salesman and an import agent. During a stint in Sydney he discovered the charms of coffee and, ever the scientist, he travelled to New Caledonia to study how the plant was grown.

Back in Wellington, he organised a company to run a coffee bar stall at the 1939–1940 Centennial Exhibition. It was a radical move when coffee à la mode was still made in the style Ukers had earlier described — from bottles of coffee essence or coffee and chicory. Hotels and restaurants served milky coffee brewed in an urn. However, while his newfangled coffee might have seemed wildly sophisticated and rather misplaced to some New Zealanders, in fact Dick Singleton's introduction of the new brew was as much a part of the exhibition's themes of progress and pioneering spirit as the dramatic displays of electricity and neon.

The exhibition ran for six months on 22 hectares of land in Rongotai, just west of Wellington airport, and the little coffee bar wooed visitors with the exotic aroma of French Maid brand coffee made from beans. It was a marketer's dream. More than 2.6 million visitors filed through the entry gates at a time when the entire population of the country numbered only 1.6 million people. With a staff of 13 working from 8.30 a.m. until 10.30 at night, Dick Singleton daily sold 200,000 cups of coffee with cream and two biscuits at 6d a time. It was, however, not an accountant's dream — at least not Dick Singleton's accountant. When the exhibition was packed up, and rents and rights had been tallied, the French Maid emerged with a profit of about £250.

Undaunted by the financial anti-climax but encouraged by the gustatory approval of his customers, Dick Singleton hired a shop on Lambton Quay and kept pouring his coffee. The profit in the first week for the first coffee house in New Zealand believed to sell pure coffee was a princely £35.

Then word got around.

With a cramped kitchen, the amiable staff led by Nell

Hook worked hard in the narrow, green-painted coffee bar to thread their way through feet and bags in order to serve the eager customers who squeezed themselves behind the wooden tables. But the service was willing and cheerful, the aromas delightful, and Dick Singleton seized the opportunity to keep everyone amused and well versed in coffee-making through his comprehensive menu.

'NOW LET'S SEE,' began the French Maid Coffee House menu of 1941, 'Our Coffee is specially blended, freshly roasted, freshly ground, several times a day.' Mr Hoy, Chief Coffee Expert for Griffiths Bros Ltd, Coffee Merchants in Sydney, added his advice for the information of the reading customer, 'Under no circumstances change your blend of "French Maid" Coffee, it is excellent.'

A brief history of coffee that romped from Kolschitzky in 17th century Vienna to Wills' Coffee House in 18th century London concluded with Bach's *Coffee Cantata* refrain, 'How sweet is the taste of coffee, more charming than a thousand kisses softer than muscatel wine'.

'Coffee was first adulterated commercially with chicory by the orders of Napoleon,' Dick Singleton instructed his captive audience. 'Chicory is an innocent and insignificant little plant; it has a long brown root which exudes a bitter juice when freshly incised. It is still an adulterant.'

There were suggestions carefully spelt out for coffee brewing at home, too, revealing 'a newer and a better way, a way in which the most flavour and aroma will be secured'. Tea got a mention as well. Broken Orange Pekoe 'specially blended for us in Ceylon' could be bought by the pot or the pound — if you must. So could French Maid Peanut Butter with 'the finest flavour of any peanut butter in Australasia'. Coffee, however, was the star. The discerning customer (who ought to take coffee black and unsweetened) could choose from:

COFFEE, with Real Cream & Biscuits 6d.
COFFEE, with Toast 9d.
COFFEE, with Crumpets and Butterscotch Sauce these are unusually delicious 9d.
COFFEE, with Canadian Doughnuts & Sauce 8d.
COFFEE, with Special Meat Pies & Bread & Butter 1/-
COFFEE, and 2 Cakes 8d.
COFFEE, and Home-made Continental Rye Bread 6d.
COFFEE, and Scones 8d.
COFFEE, and Sandwiches (practically all sandwiches are 1d. Each)
(We take special pride in the variety and quality of these. Every day there is something entirely new in our sandwiches.)
We would like you to know that all our Cakes are definitely Home-made.
Also from time to time you will find entirely new items on this menu, and you can rest assured our aim is to give you additional novelties plus quality.

The 'additional novelties' were attractions in themselves. Japanese sukiyaki, Russian borscht, Italian minestrone, Chicken Maryland, beer soup and New Zealand eel and paua made it to the tables at various times and added to the bohemian atmosphere. The French Maid became known for attracting customers from all walks of life, and offered the chance of rubbing shoulders with journalists, broadcasters and staff from the consulates, and musicians or writers who might become famous.

The French Maid also gave Wellington's emerging artists a welcome shot at fame. When the Second World War presented New Zealanders with the need to raise patriotic funds, Dick Singleton invited artists to make lightning sketches of French Maid customers and display them. Other artists provided work, and the displays changed every few weeks, developing into regular art exhibitions that charged neither hanging fees nor commissions on sales.

Dick Singleton provided his own review for *Art in New Zealand* in 1942 in the 'News from the Centres' column. 'The interesting exhibitions of paintings, drawings, etchings and the like which continually adorn the walls of the French Maid Coffee House in Wellington have been enlivened by 18 prints from the Auckland photographer, Mr L. M. Beck, Vice-President of the Auckland Camera Club' he wrote. Others who had recently exhibited included Theo Schoon, Ian Richdale,

Elizabeth Hepburn and Florence Hislop, and, reported Dick Singleton, 'sales were good'.

As passionate about the technical workings of coffee as its epicurean qualities, Dick Singleton also operated a factory at 93a Jackson Street, Petone. There, in his white chemist's coat, he roasted and ground his beans, pioneering vacuum packaging, winning the Juan Valdez Award from the Federation of Coffee Growers of Colombia and the contract to provide French Maid coffee to the Ross Sea Antarctic Expedition. It was where he made his French Maid peanut butter too, along with flapjacks he called 'Toastie Jacks', butterscotch sauce and a range of nut spreads, all exported under the trade name 'Singleton', as 'French Maid' was the name of a well known detergent sold overseas.

In 1951, the Lambton Quay building was sold, and the French Maid Coffee House was closed on Friday 7 December. Two days earlier, Dick Singleton hosted a farewell dinner for 'those who actually do the buying from us and to those who have the exasperating task of selling to us'. On the back of the menu he wrote:

For 11 years we have tried as best we could to give you extremely fast service, good food coupled with a happy, friendly service. Despite all the staff shortages etc., we ourselves have thoroughly enjoyed our efforts and we are quite sure that you also have appreciated all the barracking, back chat and other facets of the 'FRENCH

MAID'. Our thanks are due to the Artists for their co-operation. We think we have done some good for the younger generation of Artists and we only hope that in the future they find some place as satisfying to them.

Next page: The long and narrow French Maid Coffee House opened at 356 Lambton Quay in 1940 and closed in 1951. This 1940s photograph captures a typically busy, crowded daytime scene and shows the art works by local artists that were regularly displayed on the walls. (F-96756-1/2 Ms-papers-1977-01 Arthur Singleton Papers Alexander Turnbull Library, Wellington. Photographer: Leo Morel.)

FRENCH MAID

COFFEE HOUSE

No-one remembers much about the evening opening party for Suzy's Coffee Lounge on 16 August, 1964 except that, in good Dutch style, there was an abundance of flowers. The careful arrangements Suzy had already placed upstairs and downstairs were supplemented with generous, congratulatory bouquets brought by the suppliers and the tradesmen who had worked on the building. There was well-planned food, of course, and champagne and music from the old Windmill record player and general celebration.

Suzy, who had already worked a full first day, was glamorous and effervescent. Excitedly claiming selected arrivals at the door she whirled them up the stairs to the second floor where there was more air, less of a crush and a view through the large sliding windows to the Lido movie theatre across the road. Their less glossy partners she abandoned below to find their own company.

It was her finest hour. She was charming and elegant and talkative and, despite her youth, appeared to be every bit the confident Wellington businesswoman. She was in charge of the most sophisticated coffee bar in the city.

Suzy's had opened on time that morning and her staff had greeted their customers neatly dressed in black with little white aprons. Audrey Green was installed behind the till as daytime manageress, and Muriel Hoedemaeckers, wife of window-maker Theo, took over at nights. Martha Goodwin, an Irish cook who had answered Suzy's

Left: This c 1947 screen-printed menu card cover for the French Maid Coffee House was created by artist Gordon Walters. Courtesy of Margaret Orbell. (Eph-A-DINING-1947-01-cover Alexander Turnbull Library, Wellington.)

newspaper advertisement, was firmly established in the kitchen, where she would work for the next 23 years.

Together with Audrey Green and her recipe books, Suzy had chosen the food the coffee bar would serve. It was essential, she had decided, that it all be fresh and healthy. The refrigerated salad bar would take care of hygiene. The whole eating experience had to impress. The standard local fare of club sandwiches, apple squares and asparagus rolls, was unthinkable. Customers would be seduced by a sumptuous smorgasbord at lunchtime, and perfectly cooked steaks, goulashes, curries, and Wiener schnitzel in the evenings. Everyone would be treated to a refreshingly different type of service.

The coffee bar had none of the stiff formality of the restaurants around town with their crisp white tablecloths and table settings. At Suzy's the tables remained stylishly bare, and customers, instead of ordering while seated, were encouraged to take a plate from the counter, point out their salad selections from the display in the refrigerated bar and indicate whether they preferred a steak or another of the dishes du jour.

They accepted a table number, paid Audrey Green, who included a witty — or risqué, depending on the customer — observation with the change, and were seated, usually by the gracious Suzy. Their plates went on into the kitchen, the steak was cooked to specification and the completed order was delivered by a smiling waitress.

There were ham, salamis, frankfurters, croquettes, little pizzas and bratwurst to choose from, and the salads were a specialty. Audrey Green was not in the business of boring her customers. Make them unique and keep them changing, she advised. New combinations such as carrot and raisin appeared along with apple and walnut, and were dressed in a mayonnaise enriched with a slick of oil and just the right amount of piccalilli.

The coffee for a coffee bar with European influence had to be extra good too; so Suzy, since the days of the Windmill, had taken her specifications to local coffee factory Fagg's. Her coffee, she determined, would be different.

When Tom had arrived in Wellington in the 1960s it had seemed almost impossible to buy a decent cup of coffee in Wellington. While some Italian espresso machines had been imported in the 1950s — like the one Suzy had operated in the Bamboo restaurant in Invercargill — they were expensive and, because of their continuous use required skilful tune-ups and maintenance every three months. Import restrictions that followed the Black Budget of 1958 meant that many of the impressive, shiny, steaming machines that were overworked and in want of new parts were now lying silent and idle throughout the country. The simpler alternative for coffee bars was the Cona coffee system.

For the many Wellington émigrés who craved the espresso they knew from home, the answer was to buy their own beans to grind and brew from Mr and Mrs Bay whose little store in Majoribanks Street sold salamis and pickled herrings as well. Later James Smith began importing coffee beans and purchased a grinding machine.

Alfred Fagg, who had established his shop in Cuba Street in 1926, was a canny promoter and was known to scatter freshly roasted coffee beans on the footpath outside the shop, luring inside the passersby who had crushed the aromatic beans underfoot. He displayed a seven-pound coffee roasting machine in the shop window and the exotic perfumes of freshly roasted beans wafted through the door and, caught in the breezes of Cuba Street, announced coffee's presence to the city.

It had taken six weeks for Suzy, working with the technicians at the Fagg's factory, to be satisfied with the blend. The technicians would grind the beans and make a Cona brew for her each morning. For days she had sampled and tested, swilled and swallowed until she decided it was perfect. It was a European-style mix of Brazilian Fiesta, Dark Continental and European beans, ground each morning and made with a pinch of salt in strictly monitored Cona coffee pots. It was the taste of Europe that she remembered. The brew had to be fresh and punchy, and if either of the two glass pots had stood even five minutes longer than prescribed — out its contents went. Impressed with both the resulting blend and Suzy's style and aplomb, the Fagg's management team proposed marketing the blend under her name. 'Thank you, but no,' she replied. The secret blend now belonged to Suzy's.

Audrey Green's library yielded recipes for complex, dark chocolate cakes and crisp, sweet appelflaps. For Suzy, who had learned to cook by watching Hendrikus and Annie, the act of following a written recipe was a novelty.

Delectable European cheesecakes and almond cakes made at home by night manageress Muriel Hoedemaeckers, were delivered in brown paper bags. Other delicacies were ordered from Dutch couple André and Ann Jacobs at Hollandia Bakeries.

Audrey Green was influential in deciding on prices too. 'Suzy,' she would scold, 'you don't charge enough for that.' So Suzy would return to the accounts, add up all the costs and apply more realistic prices. It wasn't cheap, and some customers grumbled — but they always came back.

Her staff members might have had more experience under their belts than she did, but it was 25-year-old Suzy who gave the orders and there would be no nonsense. Waitresses who were slow or distracted were given a loud and public dressing-down regardless of who was listening. It gave her something of a reputation in Wellington as a 'sergeant-major' but, as she had done in Albergen, Suzy paid good wages and expected top performance. Her staff respected her and learnt a great deal about hard work and clean ashtrays.

So too did the Air New Zealand cabin crews who were sent to Suzy's as part of their training. Installed at a booked table, groups of aspiring air hostesses observed, analysed and noted down the speedy, efficient workings of the coffee bar. The service was particularly smart on Air New Zealand training week.

But Suzy was here, there and everywhere every day and

every night. She greeted customers, assisted the waitresses and lent a hand behind the counter when required. It was her role to maintain the flow of customers, food and staff within the confined space. If passersby hesitated at the sight of so much crowded busyness, Suzy was at the door. 'There's a lovely soup today. Plenty of room,' and she would push everyone along.

You have to be right on the spot every minute,' she instructed her staff.

Together they cleared the tables. If people got up, the table had to be wiped clean. If the waitress was upstairs, Suzy was down.

'You have to be constant,' she said.

Toasted sandwiches and *uitsmijters* were ordered all day and had to be out pronto.

Suzy was the sergeant-major — up, out, up, out. Customers didn't have much time. They wanted a meal and had to get back to work or meet an appointment or see a movie. The whole operation had to be quick and smart.

One evening the coffee bar was even busier than usual. Orders were flying in; meals were zooming out. And Suzy's patience was running thin.

'Stop yapping,' she told Tom, who was hot and rushed while cooking a series of steaks and had paused to speak to a waitress.

'One day, I'm going to walk out,' threatened Tom.

'If you walk out that door, you walk out forever. I shut it behind you and you can forget about the shop,' Suzy flashed back.

Tom walked out.

There was silence. The customers looked on in awe.

Tom walked back in.

The customers breathed again, returned to their meals and business continued as normal.

The hours were punishing too. It was like the Windmill all over again. Suzy would be at the markets early piling fresh produce into her Mercedes, securing crates on the roof rack and delivering it all to the coffee bar before going upstairs to shower and dress. Tom would go downstairs and open up early in the morning and get things ready before the rest of the staff who arrived at eight. He would stay to have a cup of coffee with Suzy when she came downstairs at 10 to take over, groomed, carefully dressed and manicured, with make-up, nail polish and jewellery and the upright bearing of success. At five in the evening Tom came back to the coffee bar to cook the steaks for the dinner customers.

On this small stage in Willis Street, Suzy played out her vision of Continental chic and sound business.

At the Bamboo and the Parisienne she had been required, in line with 1960s fashion dictates, to wear a skirt for work, but skirts weren't really her style. Now, as the boss, it was time to dress up. And she did.

It was the era of James Bond and *The Avengers*. Suzy was an amalgam of Pussy Galore and Emma Peel in her skinny, cat-suit or tight, shiny pants worn with high, cowboy-style gold and silver boots. She was as svelte as Twiggy and could also slide into a Benson and Hedges fashion competition outfit that was very popular with the customers. It featured a crocheted top that revealed her slim midriff, and had matching tight flared pants. Her hair was fashionably blonde and swept up in a cloud of hairspray, and sometimes she added a stunning hat. Her appearance caused a stir. Young male customers, who were completely unaware of Tom slapping steaks on the grill in the kitchen, vied for her favours, turning up night after night, grinning hopefully and drinking far too much coffee.

But while Suzy enjoyed the attention, she considered her attractiveness to be as much a part of her business strategy as the quality of the coffee, the food and the service. It was the business that came first.

Together, Tom and Suzy would lock up after the last guest left, clean up, and stack the crates into the Mercedes ready for the morning's run to the markets. After a hectic day Suzy often had a headache, and because of her height, she suffered a perennially sore back. They rarely got to bed before midnight.

'If success were easy, everybody would be successful. If moneymaking were easy, everybody would be rich,' Hendrikus had told his daughter. And she had believed him.

SUZY'S COFFEE LOUNGE LTD

108 Willis Street

have much pleasure in inviting

MR. MRS. [illegible]

to attend an

Opening Evening

at the above address

on 16 august 1964.

From 8 p.m.

Mrs. T. H. RABEL
Miss S. M. BEKHUIS

Above: After a full day of trading on 16 August 1964, Suzy's Coffee Lounge officially opened with an invitation-only evening celebration.

Right: This 1960s Benson and Hedges fashion competition outfit caused quite a stir in the coffee bar. (Photographer: Peter J. Cejnar.)

So the pattern was set.

Every morning, Tom switched the coffee bar lights on at six. The glowing window was a beacon in a shadowy, grey, city street, and early risers or night-workers wanting a cup of coffee at the least, and a chat if Tom was in the mood, began to call by regularly.

If the door was locked, they would knock insistently until he opened it. The coffee bar was warm, cosy and inviting. He made their coffee, put out the trays of cakes for the day and prepared the bread rolls — 12 x salami, 12 x cheese, 12 x egg and 12 x crayfish — and he and the customers would banter, turning the matinal air into a rich fug of coffee, cigarette smoke and repartee.

It became a regular event, and Tom built up his own early-morning clientele. There was something of the London 'penny university' coffee house about Tom's early-morning establishment, a place where the news of the day could be discussed and argued, and good coffee drunk.

Some days there were up to 50 customers before 8 a.m. Many were on their way home from night shift; others were on their way to begin a day of work. They got to know Tom, his opinions and his views on life, and they began to recognise each other. It was convivial and busy. Occasionally photographer Peter Cejnar, one of the regular customers who worked early hours at Valerie Studios around in Manners Street, would slip behind the counter and take over the serving while Tom caught up on his duties out the back.

Like many Dutchmen, Tom van der Kwast can be blunt. Most of the time he dispenses the easy charm of a good-looking man who has seen much of the world and is well satisfied with his lot, but early in the morning with work to be done, his patience was sometimes tested — particularly by customers who ordered pots of tea. There was one regular in particular who got under his skin. He was a solicitor who, every working day without fail, would turn up at Suzy's early in the morning and make his infuriating request.

Tom was grumpy. 'Get your tea somewhere else. I don't make tea. Go to the Coconut Grove. This is a coffee house, not a tea house. Why don't you drink coffee anyway?'

The solicitor would not be rattled. Every day, he ordered his cup of tea. Every day, Tom would be obliged to prepare his wooden tray — teapot, hot-water jug, milk jug, sugar, cup, serviette, saucer and spoon. The queue would grow and back up to the footpath outside. Tom's temper would fray. Tom would glower at the solicitor. The solicitor would beam happily back.

For years it was a source of wonder. Why did he keep returning? Anyone who took tea in the mornings, Tom reckoned in his European way, must be mad.

Years later, after Suzy's had closed and Tom grew accustomed to visiting other coffee bars for his morning fix, he saw the solicitor again. One morning in a busy café on Lambton Quay he spied the familiar form ahead of him in the queue. He leaned forward as the queue shortened and watched as the solicitor placed his order for a cup of coffee.

'You bastard,' Tom muttered. 'Why did you do it?'

The solicitor turned, saw him and grinned.

'It was such a good start to my day,' he said.

Suzy's daytime and evening clientele was more varied. There were morning coffee drinkers with time on their hands, office and shop workers wanting urgent takeaway toasted sandwiches and the Dutch *uitsmitjters*, serious lunchers, students, politicians, tourists and shoppers. And at night-time travellers and lovers, moviegoers from the Lido and the Majestic, cleaners, and a steady stream of taxi drivers stopped by.

There were regulars too. One group who had been forced to abandon Bart Cox's basement Café du Boulevard, when the Victoria Street building had been demolished, had, at first, transferred its daily lunchtime allegiance to the Windmill in Wakefield Street. When Suzy shifted to Willis Street, the group followed.

They were a mix of professionals — a printer, an insurance broker, quantity surveyors, an optometrist, a pharmacist, an accountant and a sprinkling of Brierley's company directors. What drew them together was a shared interest in the stock market. What attracted them to Suzy's was the sophistication, the good food, the efficient service and Suzy herself.

As regulars, they were entitled to avoid the queues, instead calling out 'the usual please' as they each approached the stairs and made their way to their customary table on the mezzanine floor along the Willis Street window. If there were customers already seated there, they would install themselves at one end of the table anyway, gradually easing the interlopers out.

'Oh, come and sit over here,' Suzy, the gracious hostess, would say smoothly to the affronted casuals. 'These people are here every day you know, come and sit here. You'll find it a bit quieter.'

And the stock market gang would settle down and tuck into their cheese and ham toasted sandwiches and grumble about Suzy's prices, discuss how best to manipulate the stock market and, as befitted valued regulars, paid at the counter as they left for an afternoon of work.

They were a lively lot. In the Café du Boulevard days, four of them had once won a car in a raffle, sold their prize and cashed it into one thousand one-dollar notes. They had tied the notes into a wad, suspended it from a thread and dangled the whole lot out of the window onto Victoria Street. When passersby bent to pick up the bundle from the footpath, they jerked the string away amid gales of laughter.

It was still years before the 1987 stock market crash.

On a good day there were 13 of them in the Willis Street lunch crowd; on the day Suzy's closed, they marked the occasion with champagne and had their photograph taken for the newspaper.

When they weren't in residence at Suzy's, the upstairs space was more subdued.

There were the in-between groups — before or after lunch

and before or after dinner — who met for a coffee, a snack and conversation. There were groups of serious students, and others who had aspirations to appear intellectual, who gathered to solve the problems of the world over coffee and cakes.

'Little do you know how hard life is — real life,' thought Suzy to herself as she whisked by smiling and gathering dirty plates from the tables and snippets of conversation from the air.

Artist Rita Angus came regularly and sat at her own table deep in discussion with groups of friends.

'Suzy, I'd like to do a drawing of you,' she once said.

'No, no. I don't want it. Don't put me on paper.'

So instead Rita Angus in 1967 painted the view she enjoyed from her usual seat on the mezzanine. In her painting, groups of customers are seated at the stock market lunch crowd's table against the windows that looked down to Willis Street. There is an eerie echo in the painting of Suzy's earliest impressions of New Zealanders that she had gathered when she had first arrived. In *At Suzy's Coffee Lounge*, one woman wears a pink hat, though unadorned by flowers, another is dressed in blue. The men are in black suits, but there are no tin lunch boxes.

Rita Angus admired the sleek, modern lines of Fritz Eisenhofer's design, and once remarked that she found the composition for the painting 'ready-made' at Suzy's. In notes she made for an exhibition she said the the painting was 'a composition based on the vertical and horizontal of contemporary life'.

All kinds of people came and went, crowding in and out the door, day after day, week after week, and year after year. Politicians and cleaners: taxi drivers and lovers. To Suzy they were all her customers who paid well to be served quickly and efficiently, and she treated each of them with the same level of graciousness. 'Three pence for the coffee and one shilling for the smile,' one client regularly joked. They all knew who she was, remembered her for years afterward and still greet her in the streets.

She knows hardly any of them by name.

On Saturday 16 September 1967 Tom and Suzy were married. There had been general surprise and some consternation at the prospect among the regular customers. Tom had been married before and had fathered a child; he was much older, was more experienced and sophisticated, and didn't seem the type to settle down, they muttered to themselves. Suzy had a Catholic background, Tom was Protestant; Suzy was from the country, Tom from the city. Suzy, they believed, for all her flamboyant dress and business success was in many ways still inexperienced and vulnerable. Her customers liked her and felt a need to protect her.

Suzy, hard at work behind the counter or wiping down tables and replacing ashtrays was unaware of their concern. It was all going to be a bit of a rush.

On Friday night, she raced to James Smith's department store in Cuba Street and bought a hat, gloves, shoes and nylons. At the Gold Room Boutique she bought a coat dress. They were married at 4 p.m. the next day.

The *Evening Post* described the event in detail:

Two Dutch residents, well-known in Wellington business circles, were married at the Wesley Church, Taranaki Street, recently.
The bride was Miss Susanna Maria Bekhuis, tenth daughter of the late Mr and Mrs H. W. Bekhuis, of Almelo, Holland, and the bridegroom Mr Anton Rens van der Kwast, younger son of Mrs A N van der Kwast of Amsterdam, and the late Mr van der Kwast.

The Rev Penham officiated. The bride has been in New Zealand for seven years and the groom for 15. An A-line coat-dress of cream pure silk with double buttoning and a scarf neckline was worn by the bride. Her hat was of stitched fabric in coffee and cream tones, with brim rolled at the sides and she wore coffee-brown shoes and handbag. The best man was Mr John Bekhuis of Upper Hutt.
Some 100 friends attended a cocktail party early in the evening at 'Suzy's' Coffee Lounge and a wedding dinner was held later at the White Heron Lodge.

On Sunday morning after the wedding, having assembled the filled rolls and swept their section of the Willis Street footpath, Suzy and Tom sat down together for a cup of coffee. They looked at each other across the table and burst out laughing. What had they done?

Right: Tom and Suzy van der Kwast married on 16 September 1967. (Photographer: Greig Royle Studio.)

Letting Go

Suzy was four months pregnant before she was sure that there was a baby on the way. At eight months she tripped on the stairs while working, and fell. It was 10.30 at night when her waters broke but there was no sign of any contractions. Unperturbed, she went upstairs to the flat, where she showered, manicured and polished her fingernails, and carefully did her hair so that she would look her best, before an extremely nervous Tom was allowed to drive his sufficiently well-groomed young wife to hospital. Bart Willem Hendrikus van der Kwast arrived at 5.30 the next morning.

Despite her initial nonchalance, the birth of her child weakened Suzy considerably. Always pressed for time, she had only just enrolled in an antenatal class and hadn't made it to the first session before Bart was born. Unprepared, she was nervous about caring for her little son, but her maternal instincts took over, and any knowledge and experience that was lacking was more than compensated for by the new and unexpected maternal love that welled inside her. Her Plunket nurse was on hand to fill any gaps.

Tom and Suzy kept up their punishing routine, neatly fitting the little baby and his requirements into their usual activities. Night manageress Muriel Hoedemaeckers collected Bart mid-morning from the coffee bar and cared for him at her home in Island Bay during the day. She would return him when she began work, Suzy would take over and go upstairs to the flat, and Tom would take over steak-cooking duties for the evening shift.

Right: Suzy and Bart van der Kwast in 1968.

Baby Bart, however, had his own specific requirements. For his first two years he slept poorly and had repeated nose bleeds, and his young mother became increasingly tired. The work continued, and Suzy struggled on. It was not until Bart was a toddler that a visiting surgeon discovered the problem with his nasal passages and carried out an almost instantly successful operation. With a safely sleeping child, at last there was some reprieve.

However, there was more loneliness to contend with. At a low ebb after childbirth and with her hormones in a tizzy, Suzy missed her family deeply. On the other side of the world from her sisters, she felt isolated and alone, and there were doubts and many tears.

On top of her distress, it had become apparent that with a baby to care for and accommodate, the flat was growing too small, and Tom and Suzy began the hunt for a larger house. In 1969 they shifted to their new home in Evans Bay. It was spacious and comfortable, and the wide view of the bay settled Suzy's nerves.

There was a down side, though. The coffee bar had become much more than just a job; it was Suzy's life. Now there was no waitress or manageress on a break to climb the stairs for a gossip with Suzy and to amuse Bart, and no busy hum of the coffee bar drifting upstairs. There were neighbours at Evans Bay but they were older, and Suzy felt they had no interest in a young, foreign mother with a baby.

By the time Bart was three years old, Suzy was perilously thin and exhausted.

'Take a holiday,' her doctor ordered, 'or I'll put you in hospital.'

So she took his advice. Tom and Bart went south to stay with her family, the Evans Bay house was let and temporary managers took responsibility for the coffee bar. Suzy returned to the Netherlands not flying her own plane, as Hendrikus had once hoped, but as successful a businesswoman as he would ever have wanted, and with more motivation than just rest and recuperation.

There was another task that needed to be dealt with. It was one that had gnawed away at her for years and which, she suspected, now contributed to her current physical weakness.

When Suzy was six years old it had become clear to everyone that her mother was very ill and required rest and calm. In order to relieve the pressure on the busy and crowded household four of the youngest children were sent to live with relatives.

It was a disastrous move for Suzy. Away from her family, confused and homesick, she was preyed on for months by an adult cousin. For a little girl who had grown up with older brothers, it was an appalling breach of trust. Frightened and disturbed by the betrayal, Suzy finally clung to Hendrikus on one of his weekly visits and told him what she was being forced to do. The reaction was swift and decisive. Suzy's clothes were gathered into a sack on the back of the bicycle, and her father took her home.

The incident had remained a secret from friends and family, but the memories had lurked in her mind ever since and hovered menacingly between her and her boyfriends. When Bart was born they had flooded back. Now 32 years old, Suzy returned to the Netherlands and confronted the man. She had suffered all her life because of his evil actions, she told him calmly. She did not intend to suffer any longer. He wept. She left.

In many ways the Netherlands was not the place she remembered. There were far more houses, the people had different attitudes, drugs were easily available and sold in 'coffee' houses, and the Dutch now lived a much more carefree life. But it was not Suzy's life, she decided. She had grown apart from it all. It had taken her seven sometimes hard and often lonely years, she reckoned, to settle properly in her new country and now, 11 years on, she felt like a real New Zealander.

Message delivered, job done, considerably strengthened both physically and emotionally, she returned home to Wellington.

If there had been any animosity shown by other proprietors towards the newest coffee bar on the block, Suzy hadn't noticed it. She had been far too busy. Besides, she reckoned, each coffee bar had always had its own stamp and its own clientele, and there was certainly room for her own.

The styles of the coffee bars were many and varied, and were the work, according to Rob MacGregor, of proprietors-cum-amateur psychologists:

... they know that the average public want to escape the dry surroundings of everyday life. They also know that the make believe attitude that lies dormant within a person's mind responds quickly to surroundings that are given a make believe setting.

Like 'Alice in Wonderland' or 'Robin Hood', the background of fantasy gets under our skin and leaves us with the feeling that our minds are on the same plane as the book. A likewise feeling is experienced when one enters a coffee lounge. Perhaps the decor may be Oriental, Latin American, artistically modern, or eerily quaint; then again a shipboard atmosphere may be created by murals depicting ships at sea, a Pacific Island background, or even an aquarium setting ... the staff of New Zealand coffee lounges are, if to be taken on the whole, composed of fifty per cent recent arrivals from Europe. The recent arrivals, mostly Dutch and Hungarian, prior to their arrival in this country had probably never seen the inside of a coffee lounge before, but by the simple expedient of taking a menu order with a continental touch and by introducing a Hollywood butler style, they have set a standard that New Zealanders have been quick to appreciate. A slight movement of a chair for madam to sit down, a pleasant 'Good evening, Sir,' and a steady flick of a lighter for a guest's cigarette, have all aided in the coffee lounge atmosphere. The local boy and girl who prior to entering a coffee lounge had only seen continental waiters on a movie screen could now see them in the flesh, and once again the proprietor came out on top with his amateur psychology.

The Casa Fontana around in Victoria Street offered discreet live music with its coffee, and a fountain lit by a green light. In 1958, six Sunday evening jazz concerts held in the coffee bar and organised by the Wellington Musician's Club were recorded for radio by the New Zealand Broadcasting Service.

Further up Victoria Street, the Mexicali was loud with jazz and, along with the Sorrento, enjoyed a certain cachet following their prosecution by the city council for allowing dancing on the premises on a Sunday. The Mexicali stayed open until 3 a. m. and attracted into its already crowded, gloomy interior — along with bearded men in dark glasses, and women with long hair — customers dawdling in the city after the movies and hoping for adventure.

Down in Massey House on 126–132 Lambton Quay, in the coffee bar above Roy Parson's elegant book shop, Harry Seresin and his mother had early been inducting Wellingtonians into the skills of lingering longer over a cup of coffee with, perhaps, cheesecake, the newly-introduced yoghurt and Russian rye-bread sandwiches. The café-bookshop arrangement celebrated coffee, good books and classical music in European style. It was here that theatre people nurtured their dreams to form Downstage Theatre, where Harry Seresin was financial director for nine years.

Eight-storey Massey House was designed by Austrian-born architect Ernst Plischke and his partner Cedric Firth in 1952 for the Meat and Dairy marketing boards, and was built by A. G. Wells. When it opened in 1957, many people were suspicious of its international style; others hailed it as the first truly Modernist office building in New Zealand. The ground floor foyer, which also provided the entrance to the bookshop, was paved with Italian marble, and the glass curtain walls and main door with its massive panes of glass earned it the nickname 'the Crystal Building'.

Coffee bar patrons ascended the 'floating' stairway to Harry Seresin's gallery-style coffee bar on the mezzanine, which was lined with panels of rimu and sycamore veneer and hung with original art works. Although only about half its original size, and without the original view down to the book shop and out to Lambton Quay, the coffee bar today remains much the same.

Next page: Parsons Books and Harry Seresin's coffee bar above it opened in 1957 in Massey House at 126–132 Lambton Quay. This photograph and the one following were probably taken in that year. (PAColl-2460-1-27 Harry Seresin Collection Alexander Turnbull Library, Wellington. Photographer: George Kolhap.)

ROY PARSONS

Above: In this stylish coffee bar Harry Seresin introduced yoghurt and other Continental foods to many Wellingtonians. (PAColl-2460-1-25 Harry Seresin Collection Alexander Turnbull Library, Wellington. Photographer: George Kolhap.)

On the corner of Roxburgh and Majoribanks streets the Monde Marie, ruled by colourful Mary Seddon, former teacher at Samuel Marsden Collegiate and film critic for *Truth*, and granddaughter of past Liberal Party premier Richard John Seddon, attracted an educated, bohemian crowd. An adventurer who had travelled solo through Europe for four years, she returned to what she perceived as comparatively dull Wellington in 1950 with a mission to provide the city with a Continental-style meeting place where customers could talk and listen to music. The coffee bar opened in 1958.

She persuaded international stars to perform at Monde Marie including Austrian-born actor and folk singer Theodore Bikel, American singer-songwriter Tom Lehrer, Indian sitarist and composer Ravi Shankar, American folk singer Judy Collins, Paul Stookey and Mary Travers of folk group Peter Paul and Mary, and American singer-guitarist Josh White. New Zealand performers, many of whom were paid one dollar per hour with free food, included Peter Cape, Terry Bryant, Barry Crump, Nick Villard, Mike Stebbings, Richard Mills, Helen Phare and Craig Berry. Local folksingers worked in the kitchen for free coffee, food and a chance to perform. The permanent black-stockinged and short-skirted waitresses in 'Mary's purdah' were guarded carefully by her and delivered home safely after work.

The emphasis at the Monde Marie was on music and conversation, not food or coffee; but it provided its patrons with cheap and simple curry and rice, spaghetti bolognaise and a plat du jour — most often chilli con carne — with salad and a bread roll and cheesecake to follow, all for a dollar. The decor included the popular fishing nets strung from the ceiling and candles stuffed into wax-encrusted Chianti bottles.

Young, black-clad women with pale, frosted lipsticks, generous eyeliner and false eyelashes squeezed into the coffee bar with their male counterparts, who were clad in stove-pipe jeans and often sported beards. Everyone wore boots. Conversation flowed freely between numbers — you had to talk to your neighbour when you were practically sitting on his knee — and so did the Cona coffee often laced with alcohol and served in dark brown mugs made by local potter Helen Mason. A signature chorus was 'Whisky in the Jar', which was sung lustily — and frequently — by all present.

Mary Seddon fought unsuccessfully for years for her own wine licence. She was protective of her patch, scathing of other coffee bars and fiercely critical of any competitors — including Suzy, whose coffee, she once grumpily claimed, was 'so cheap, it was probably only Kenyan'.

The Balladeer Coffee Bar in upper Willis Street, run by Frank and Mary Fyfe, and the Chez Paree upstairs in the Embassy Theatre building, entered via a fake cave, were other crowded venues for folk singers and their young fans, who were duffle-coated and mini-skirted (and 'less hip', according to Mary Seddon and the Monde Marie crowd). The Balladeer, which originally seated its customers on palliasses on the floor, later graduated to wooden forms and trestle tables for audiences and kitchen stools for performers, and nurtured the beginnings of the Wellington Folk Club. The Dutch Tulip in Herbert Street was a hangout for poets, including, at one time, James K. Baxter. The Capri Coffee Lounge was on Manners Street.

Above: Rod Mackinnon and Dave Hollis perform at the Monde Marie c 1968. The coffee bar, opened 10 years earlier by Mary Seddon on the corner of Roxburgh and Majoribanks streets, dispensed music and serious conversation along with coffee. (Ep-industry-restaurants-m-r-01 Dominion Post Collection Alexander Turnbull Library, Wellington.)

Other notable coffee bars sported equally lyrical names. The Picasso, La Scala, Sans Souci Coffee Shoppe, Sorrento, Coconut Grove, Man Friday, Tête à Tête, the Jolly Frog and the Rendez-Vous (near the entrance to Cable Car Lane) were all once on Lambton Quay. The Buttery, which was at first on Lambton Quay, shifted to nearby Woodward Street; the Downtown Club was on Jervois Quay; the Psychedelic Id was on Majoribanks Street; and the Oracle on Cornhill Street.

Above: This trade card signals the presence of the Woodward Buttery — a coffee and tea house located at No. 7 Woodward Street in the 1970s. (Eph-a-dining-1970s-01 Alexander Turnbull Library, Wellington.)

There were many other coffee bars that came and went.

By the end of the 1960s there were more than 60 coffee shops, coffee bars or coffee lounges in the central Wellington area, often sited upstairs or downstairs in basements in an attempt both to achieve an ambience of intimacy and to avoid the higher rents of footpath-entry premises.

In 1967 there was a new and startlingly different face on the block. Carmen's International Coffee Lounge at 86 Vivian Street, in a former clothing factory with a four-bedroom flat upstairs and next door to the Salvation Army headquarters, was presided over by Wellington's best-known transsexual, who had recently returned from Sydney. Beyond the assertively Oriental facade the exotic interior positively glowed, with its red-painted walls hung with red, plush velvet curtains, Oriental rugs and prints, and its ruby-red carpet. Above an old wooden mantelpiece was a huge mirror; there were tropical fish cruising in a tank, a piano and a juke box, a parrot in a bamboo cage, three Siamese cats and generous arrangements of grasses and peacock feathers. Carmen's was gorgeous.

The International Coffee Lounge was licensed to seat 80 people at its polished mahogany and teak tables, but on a good night it was bulging. Tea, soft drinks, toasted sandwiches, cakes, pastries and scones were served, and coffee invariably included a nip of brandy. Most of the food came from Martin Yee's shop nearby, but the highly praised chocolate walnut cake and the pastries were bought from Suzy's Coffee Lounge and passed off as Carmen's own.

The establishment was more than a coffee lounge, it was Carmen's 'theatre' for 13 years and it was geared for an impressive performance.

In her memoirs she refers to her waiting staff as 'hostesses' and describes how she hired only those 'boys' and 'girls' whom she considered to be attractive. With the exception of those assistants who were lesbian, all the hostesses were male, though sometimes it was difficult to tell. They all wore big wigs, fluttered luxuriant eyelashes, flaunted low necklines and jangled large earrings, and were expected not only to glide around serving food and drink but also to pause and chat with the customers. There was sex on the menu too, and customers were encouraged to signal their sexual preference through a ritual known as 'the cups'. To arrange straight sex with a hostess, a client would turn his coffee cup upside down on the saucer; for a transvestite, a transsexual or a drag queen, the cup was placed on its side; for gay sex, the saucer went on top of the cup.

At first Carmen's opened at eight in the morning and closed at three in the afternoon. Once its presence was well and truly noted, the hours were changed; the doors opened at six in the evening and on most nights the coffee house stayed open until six the next morning.

Some Wellingtonians loved Carmen's; others hated everything about it. It was loud and uncompromising, outrageous and edgy. There were fights sometimes and police raids, windows were smashed by disaffected clients and paint splattered by the outraged. Carmen kept a donated radio permanently switched to the police radio band and a buzzer under the counter behind a pile of cups that warned prostitutes and clients upstairs in the event of an unexpected incursion.

Right: Wellington's early coffee bars were regarded by some people as the domain of the city's beatnik culture as this 1960s drawing by an unknown artist demonstrates. (B-074-080 Alexander Turnbull Library, Wellington.)

LAMBTON QUAY

In the seventies everything changed.

Leading the trend, in 1970 the doors of the Monde Marie were closed for good. Mary Seddon ascribed the waning popularity of her coffee bar to the growing affluence of the city. Young people who had their own flats — and, more significantly, shared them with their partners — had no need of a dark and crowded meeting place where no-one would look askance at passion. Other coffee bars felt the same slump in patronage and quickly followed suit. The golden era of Wellington's coffee bars was almost over.

The *New Zealand Listener* had already predicted their demise, and Caliban, writing in 1957, had wept at the prospect:

'La Giaconda' when you see it at noon is just concrete walls draped in muslin, and your waiter isn't French but Dutch with a French accent, and the concoction masquerading under the elegant name of Cappuccino is probably American blend buried beneath an excess of synthetic cinnamon. So we have to admit that there's an element of spoof in the whole thing.

Is there, however, something else behind it? For instance, have New Zealanders decided they like coffee — that tea is not only the cheapest drink in the world, but also the dullest? It's no doubt true that hitherto we have tended to identify 'coffee' with the liquid which goes under that name on railway stations, and which is apparently meant to keep travellers on the Main Trunk in a state of appreciative wakefulness. Inevitably then, there are new devotees. Thus we also have to admit that a lot of this rage is genuine. Yet I venture to suggest that 'La Giaconda' would keep open even if her coffee cups were filled with vinegar, and her South American open sandwiches with seaweed. You could strip the fishnet off the walls, insist that the waiter drop his langue d'oil, burn every poster, break every disc, but 'La Giaconda' would still remain.

For it seems likely that New Zealand has found, apart from a new fad and a new drink, a new tongue. In 'La Giaconda' you may discuss Suez, the state of three per cents, or the length of your neighbour's hair. And if you're alone you can listen in quite well to someone else talking about Rilke or the condition of the roads.

It is perhaps too hopeful to think that New Zealand will benefit the world by belching forth a crop of latter-day philosophies, but she may benefit herself by helping to make leisure and leisured talk institutions instead of luxuries. On the other hand, this diagnosis may be wrong. The hopes expressed may be frustrated. Red ink may be destined shortly to become de rigueur in her ledgers, but for me, long may 'La Giaconda' smile.

Changes to the liquor laws in the 1960s also hastened the decline in coffee bar patronage. They brought significant social change to New Zealand and challenged the exclusive popularity of the coffee bar scene. Until 1961, alcohol could not be served with food except in hotels. With the change in regulations, restaurants thrived.

The compulsory six o'clock closing of bars ended in 1967.

The 'six o'clock swill' had been a leftover mechanism from days when drinking had been at worst incapacitating and at best immoderate. The restrictions were introduced as a temporary war measure in 1917 and became a permanent fixture in 1918. There had been pressure also to clamp down on drinking altogether when, in the following year, 49.7 per cent of the population voted for prohibition. Ironically, the restrictions had encouraged the kind of drinking they had been put in place to destroy. Aware they had only a few hours of the evening in which to consume alcohol, many pub drinkers used the time to pour booze down their throats. At 6 p.m. they decanted on to the streets drunk, noisy and often aggressive.

The 1967 change to the law to allow bars to stay open until 10 at night meant much more than just the eradication of the early evening binge drinking. It brought somewhat improved drinking habits, encouraged women to enter the more civilised drinking places, enabled bars to serve food and introduced new venues that could serve drink, including the supermarket-sized and noisy 'booze barns' with their accommodatingly huge car parks.

The effects on the coffee bars were mixed. During their first year of trading, while six o'clock-closing was still in force, Tom and Suzy had routinely sat by the locked coffee bar door in the evenings opening it only to customers who clearly were not intoxicated. Finally they had got the message through that Suzy's was not an establishment for rowdy evening drunks. Closing-up had always been a dangerous business, but the concentration of drinking to beat the clock had made unruly crowds a regular feature of the city's streets. Suzy's would not mourn the death of the six o'clock swill.

However, the introduction of food to bars brought less welcome change to the coffee bar trade. Where once only the coffee bars were open for refreshments after the movies, now moviegoers had the choice of an evening drink and a snack. And Wellingtonians' newly acquired sophisticated tastes in varied and fresh food — nurtured to a large extent by Suzy's Continental cuisine and developed with greater affluence and wider travel — led to higher expectations of dining and a graduation from coffee bars to the new restaurants that could also stay open until late.

Wellington was becoming adventurous. Chinese restaurants had been operating throughout the country since 1960, and Indian restaurants, once the exclusive dining venue for Indian New Zealanders, had become popular haunts for all. Ambitious home cooks, too, were experimenting with rice, pasta, spices, yoghurt, sour cream, aubergines and courgettes, and that most revolutionary addition to the bland Kiwi diet — garlic.

There was fast food to be had too. Hamburger bars were established in the city by the mid-1960s, and Porirua laid claim to the first McDonald's in 1976.

Television was becoming common place, and Graham Kerr's cooking programme was beamed to a fascinated audience of hitherto unsophisticated and cholesterol vulnerable palates. Breath and blood tests applied to drivers suspected of being drunk were phased in with 10 p.m. closing. Going out at night was losing something of its allure.

Within a few years the coffee bars had all but disappeared and the exotic names vanished from shop frontages in Courtenay Place and on Lambton Quay.

But in Willis Street Suzy's continued to prosper.

There was still business to be had for a high-class coffee bar, and Suzy's — still open from 7 a.m. until 9 p.m. seven days a week except Christmas Day — was doing well.

From the very first days of the coffee bar's operations the till had been heavy with real money — notes and coins not plastic cards — which had to be counted carefully at nights. After work on Sundays, tired and companionably quiet after the commotion of the day, Suzy and Tom would sort all the cash ready for banking. It was dirty work, and their hands would be black after the task was complete. On some nights, guests at the Evans Bay house helped out. No money-counting; no roast dinner.

It wasn't easy money to come by. The customers kept pouring through the doors and the work never let up, but some people, Suzy figured, never recognised the effort required. Once when one of her cheques had been declined at her bank she grew very angry. It was a busy time in the school holidays, with endless streams of tired mothers and noisy, famished children. She gathered the week's takings — eight big, brown bags full of money — stuffed them all into one bag and stormed down the road. 'Here,' she told the alarmed ANZ manager. 'You count it and bank it. I haven't got time. I'm too busy making money.' Then she dumped the money on the floor and stormed back to Suzy's. She was the talk of the town.

Eventually there was enough in the coffers for Suzy, Tom and Bart to take time out and travel overseas. They left the coffee bar in the capable hands of Swiss couple Hans and Josy Sten, who ran it so precisely that few people knew the van der Kwasts were absent.

Above and right: In the 1970s, many of Wellington's coffee bars closed following changes to the liquor laws, new dining habits and growing affluence in the capital. Suzy's continued trading busily until the McGill's Building, which required extensive strengthening against earthquake risk, was sold.

Meanwhile Tom, with his real estate hat on, had contingency plans under way. For three years he had been persuading the owners of the neighbouring buildings to sell their properties to him. There were 12 different owners and at first many of them were not interested in parting with their titles, but it was a time when real estate was not doing so well, and eventually they all agreed to sell. The total sum paid for the wedge of buildings from Boulcott Street to the Majestic Theatre was $1.3 million.

It was a risky business. For one whole year there was no buyer in sight for the block of land and, even with loans and the steady income from Suzy's, Tom realised he would need a partner. The partner arrived by chance in the coffee bar, but Dutchman Tom, who had lived through the hardships of the war and had never forgotten them, was resistant. The millionaire who was keen to join him was German.

Tom weighed the situation carefully. Maybe they could keep the land and lease it, or perhaps they could sell it as one lump. In the end, the partnership was sealed and the deal was done. The building was tired and Suzy's needed serious refurbishing. A 1972 building report had classified McGill's Building as a Class A earthquake risk, preventing further major alterations and requiring either demolition or significant strengthening within 10 years. It was the end of an era.

Tom and his German partner sold the land and buildings to an Auckland investor for $9 million, and the McGill's building, along with its neighbours, was demolished in 1987. The triangular site later became the Majestic Centre — the tallest building in Wellington and described by the *National Business Review* in 1991 as 'star quality architecture'. The comprehensive Rainbow development, designed by Manning and Associates, included a three-level podium area, a 30-storey tower block and an underground car park.

But there was a rider in the contract and a surprise in the development. Tom, with his European heritage, his fondness for old buildings and his hearty respect for character and history, insisted that one old house on the Boulcott Street site be retained. It belonged to Wellington, he decided. The old 'House of Ladies' or 'Henry Pollen House' as it was variously known had been a doctor's rooms, a dental surgery and more famously a pink-painted brothel, and it deserved to live on. Discussions were held. Plans were drawn. Arrangements were made and the Victorian villa at No. 12 Boulcott Street was duly shifted and today pins the corner of Boulcott and Willis streets in a gesture of cheerful defiance to its towering, modern neighbour.

Tom and Suzy had leased out the coffee bar operation for its last year to Margaret Verhoeven and had shifted to Brisbane to be with Bart, who was now studying at university. Suzy had dabbled in real estate, and they had travelled extensively — and expensively — overseas, returning to Wellington early in 1987.

MARCH
MARCH
Suzy's
COFFEE LOUNGE

Left: Demolition begins in 1987 on the Willis Street buildings to make way for the new Majestic Centre.
Above: The Evening Post *recorded building progress on 26 February 1991.*

Coffee bar S

sell

retire

After 23 years in

moves on

Last cup

at Suzy's

wenty-three years

a luncht

zy retires

Dining habit

Coffee-bar

er cafe Suzy

Coffee-bar Suz

etires to sell

Surfers Paradis

Above: Newspaper headlines mark Suzy's retirement from the coffee house business.

For Suzy, the demise of her coffee bar was an enormous event. She had travelled a long way through time and place, and Suzy's had been her goal. She had become an important businesswoman in the adopted city that she loved. She had battled with and overcome sadness, loneliness, ill health and poverty, and had fun too.

She was the one the newspapers, magazines, radio and television came to when they needed a comment on the visit of Dutch royalty, the state of retailing in the capital, the plight of the working woman or how to keep looking young. It was Suzy that introduced Wellington to Dutch appelflaps. It was Suzy who had stood for the Wellington City and Wellington Regional councils in 1980 on the Rates Reform Association ticket. It is Suzy who is now immortalised on the walls of the Museum of Wellington City and Sea and in the archives of the city's libraries and museums.

The *Evening Post* marked her going. 'Coffee bar Suzy retires' ran the headline. 'The first lady of the Wellington coffee bar scene is retiring, but she will still keep in touch.'

The stock market lunch crowd gathered for the last time on 24 March and toasted Suzy, the coffee bar and their loyal patronage with champagne, and the *Evening Post* took their photograph. Customers trooped in, gave Suzy flowers and wished her luck. On the last day of the coffee bar's operations, Suzy made a brief speech thanking her staff members for their loyal service and left in tears.

The coffee bar in Willis Street that had reigned for 23 years had been her very own *stampcafé*; her right hand, misshapen by a lifetime of peeling potatoes and pouring coffee, remains her badge of courage. 'Success,' Hendrikus had told her, 'comes from 10 per cent luck and 90 per cent hard work.' He would have had good reason to be proud of her.

The tables, chairs and all the chattels of a coffee bar were sold and the proceeds given to charity. The doors of Suzy's shut for the last time, and a gap yawned in Willis Street.

But not for long.

Coffee houses are adaptable creatures. From the *kahwe khaneh* to the penny universities, from Florian's to the French Maid, they have evolved and survived. The moment was ripe now for a rebirth of Wellington's coffee culture.

It was time for the reign of the barista; the growth of an industry of roasting, blending and grinding; a return of the shiny, spitting, precocious Italian coffee machine; the spilling of chairs and tables onto the city's busy footpaths; and the emergence of a new and exciting coffee style.

The coffee house is dead, long live the coffee house

Bibliography

Published works:

Hutchins, Graham, *The Swinging Sixties: when New Zealand changed forever*, Harper Collins, Auckland, 2008

Hodgson, Barbara, *Italy out of hand: a capricious tour, Chronicle* Books, San Francisco, 2005

Lochore, R. A., *From Europe to New Zealand*, A. H. & A. W. Reed, Wellington, 1951

Rupe, Carmen, *Carmen: my life as told to Paul Martin*, Benton Ross Publishers Ltd., Auckland, 1988

MacGregor, Rob, *Around New Zealand in Eighty Cups*, Penrose Printing Co., Auckland, 1960

King, Michael, 'On the Purchase of Oysters, Terakihi and Trollopes', *Writing Wellington: twenty years of Victoria University Writing Fellows*, Victoria University Press, Wellington, 1999

Schouten, Hank, *Tasman's legacy: the New Zealand-Dutch connection*, New Zealand-Netherlands Foundation, Wellington 1992

Speerstra, Hylke, *Cruel Paradise: life stories of Dutch emigrants,* (trans. Henry J. Baron), Wm. B. Eerdmans Publishing Company, Grand Rapids/ Cambridge U.S., 2005

Thomson, K. W., 'The Dutch' in *Immigrants in New Zealand,* K. W. Thomson and A. D. Trlin (eds), Massey University, Palmerston North, 1970

Ukers, William H., *All About Coffee*, The Tea and Coffee Trade Journal Company, New York, second edition 1935

Weinberg, Bennett Alan and Bonnie K. Bealer, *The World of Caffeine: the science and culture of the world's most popular drug*, Routledge, New York, 2002

Warmbrunn, Werner, *The Dutch under German Occupation 1940–1945*, Stanford University Press, Stanford, California, 1963

Links:

'Overview: 1920–1950 — Wellington cafe culture', URL: http://www.nzhistory.net.nz/culture/the-daily-grind/overview-1920-1950, (Ministry for Culture and Heritage)

'Dining out – food in New Zealand', URL:http://www.nzhistory.net.nz/culture/no-pavlova-please/dining-out, (Ministry for Culture and Heritage)

'Caffé Florian', http://www.caffeflorian.com/

'M/S Johan van Oldenbarnevelt', http://www.oceanlinermuseum.co.uk/JVO%20History.htm

'MS Johan van Oldenbarnevelt', http://www.ssmaritime.com/jvoch5.htm

'A Forgotten Chapter: Holland under the Third Reich', http://www-lib.usc.

edu/~anthonya/war/main.htm
'History of immigration', Jock Phillips, Te Ara – t*he Encyclopedia of New Zealand*, http://www.TeAra.govt.nz/NewZealanders/NewZealandPeoples/HistoryOfImmigration/en
'Dutch', Redmer Yska, Te Ara – *the Encyclopedia of New Zealand,* http://www.TeAra.govt.nz/NewZealanders/NewZealandPeoples/Dutch/en

Oral histories:

Cappuccino Oral History Project, Oral History Centre, Alexander Turnbull Library of New Zealand:
Boswijk, Eelco, interviewed by Dinah Priestley, Nelson, 12 and 13 December 1993, OHC 7316
Jones, Sir Robert, 'The Rise and Fall of New Zealand's Coffee Bars in the 1950s and 60s', interviewed by Dinah Priestley, 18 November, 1993, OHC 4729 and 4730
Seddon, Mary, interviewed by Dinah Priestley, 24 September 1991, OHC 7320
Van der Kwast, Suzy, interviewed by Dinah Priestley, Wellington, 20 July 1993, OHC 7319

Newspaper and magazine articles

Aldridge, Val, 'Harry loved theatre and cafes', *The Dominion*, 13 October, 1994
Caliban, 'Found: a new pleasure', *New Zealand Listener*, 12 July, 1957
Coughlan, Kate, 'Cafe Queen', *Evening Post*, 3 January 1998
Dashfield, Prue, 'Hard work serves Suzy', *The Dominion*, 27 September 1984
Du Fresne, Karl, 'Glory days at the Monde Marie', *Evening Post*, 13 July, 2000
Du Fresne, 'Fond of the Monde', *New Zealand Listener*, 29 May, 2010
Longmore, Mary, 'Café Pioneers', *Evening Post*, 1 July, 1997
Stuart, Michael, 'Making of the Monde Marie', *Evening Post*, 28 August, 1996
Van Dongen, Yvonne, 'The Invisible Immigrants', *New Zealand Geographic*, No. 15, July-September, 1992
'Jazz at the coffee club', *New Zealand Listener*, 28 March, 1958
'Women's News', *Evening Post*, 26 September, 1967
'Coffee bar Suzy retires', *Evening Post*, 25 July, 1986
'Last cup at Suzy's', *Evening Post*, 24 March, 1987
'Serving up rates reform' *Evening Pos*t, 4 September, 1980
'Changing shape of Boulcott corner', *Evening Post*, 26 February, 1991
'Dutch royal couple welcomed to New Zealand by indigenous Maori warriors', *International Herald Tribune*, 30 October 2006

Unpublished papers:
Arthur Dick Singleton Papers, Alexander Turnbull Library, Ref. no. MS-Papers-1977
Rita Angus Papers, Alexander Turnbull Library, Ref. no. MS-Papers-1399-3/1
292 Wakefield Street, Wellington City Archives, Reg. no. 00037:18:537
292 Wakefield Street, coffee shop, Wellington City Archives, Reg no. 0058:241:C10763
108–120 Willis Street, premises papers, Wellington City Archives, Reg. no. 00009:1240:45/15/97
Health licence, 108 Willis Street, Wellington City Archives, Reg. no. 00009:294:8/1594
110–120 Willis Street, shop alterations, Wellington City Archives, Reg. no. 0058:345:C14813

Interviews:
Suzy van der Kwast and Tom van der Kwast, Wellington, 17 May, 2008
Suzy van der Kwast and Tom van der Kwast, Wellington, 10 June, 2008
Suzy van der Kwast and Tom van der Kwast, Wellington, 11 June 2008
Suzy van der Kwast and Tom van der Kwast, Wellington, 12 June 2008
Suzy van der Kwast and Tom van der Kwast, Wellington, 13 June, 2008
Suzy van der Kwast and Tom van der Kwast, Wellington, 15 July, 2008
Suzy van der Kwast and Tom van der Kwast, Wellington, 16 July, 2008
Suzy van der Kwast, Wellington, 17 July, 2008
Tom van der Kwast, Wellington 18 July, 2008
Fritz Eisenhofer and Helen Eisenhofer, Peka Peka, 27 August, 2008
Alan Perry and Luba Perry, Peka Peka, 3 November 2008
Stan Noble, Wellington, 4 November 2008
Rosalyn Hoedermaekers, Wellington, 3 November 2008
Telephone conversation Jan McGuinness, April 2009.

Index